D0934004

Classic Superbikes

Classic Superbikes

ALAN DOWDS

amber
BOOKS

This edition published in 2019

Published by
Amber Books Ltd
United House
North Road
London N7 9DP
United Kingdom
www.amberbooks.co.uk
Instagram: amberbooksltd
Facebook: www.facebook.com/amberbooks
Twitter: @amberbooks

ISBN: 978-1-78274-915-8

Project Editor: Michael Spilling
Design: Hawes Design

Printed in China

Picture credits: All photographs © Art-Tech/Aerospace, except pages 6–13 © TRH Pictures.

Contents

INTRODUCTION

For most people, apart from jet fighter pilots or Formula One racing car drivers, the most dynamic vehicular experience available is a modern superbike. The cutting edge of powered two-wheel technology offers amazing acceleration, incredible top speeds and stunning braking, with more handling finesse than 99 per cent of riders will ever use. Machines such as Yamaha's YZF-R1 have the performance parameters of a World Superbike racing machine of only a few years before, while super-fast bikes such as Suzuki's Hayabusa can reach 320km/h (200mph) in less than 30 seconds. And such performance comes for around half the price of a family saloon. It is as if a popular, mass-produced car was capable of competing in a Formula One race.

But how did motorcycling arrive at such a pinnacle of design, technology and performance? The roots for this spectacular area of automotive development are probably to be found in the ashes of the atomic bombs which were dropped on Japan in 1945, bringing an end to World War II in the east. Japan emerged from the darkness of war crippled by defeat and with much of its industrial muscle crushed by Allied bombing.

But here and there, the signs of economic renewal began to appear. Along with food and shelter, there was a great need for cheap personal transport. Cars were beyond the ability of industry to produce and of consumers to purchase, but bicycles were

The Trident Sprint 900 was one of the most successful new-generation Triumphs to emerge from the company's modern Hinckley factory in the 1990s.

TRIUMPH
Sprint

cheap, and it was only a matter of time before small engineering concerns began fitting tiny engines to bicycle-based frames. These primitive, early motorcycles helped kick-start the sluggish Japanese economy, and small-capacity, commuter-type motorcycles became the norm throughout the 1950s and early 1960s.

At that time, the British motorcycle industry was dominant, although Italian and German motorcycles were again becoming important. Firms such as BSA, Triumph, Matchless and Norton produced the mainstream motorcycles of the day. But while Japan was steadily improving its products, lack of investment and managerial foresight meant that British motorcycles remained at pretty much the same basic technology level.

Then, in 1969, came a huge shock for the British industry. Honda released its CB750, a high-performance machine that easily outclassed anything else on two wheels. The CB750's air-cooled eight-valve overhead-cam four-cylinder engine was a marvel for the time, and its arrival signalled the beginning of the end for British dominance of the world of motorcycle design.

Throughout the 1970s, this trend continued. Japan continued to produce landmark machines, and Kawasaki's Z1 900cc (55ci) four-stroke, Suzuki's two-stroke triples and Yamaha's two-stroke twins steadily increased performance, reliability and styling. Meanwhile, the manufacturing crisis of the 1970s meant that UK manufacturers slowly went out of business.

By 1984, the Japanese had a stranglehold on motorcycle production. And then Kawasaki released a model which arguably defined the future course of sportsbike development, the GPZ900R Ninja. The GPZ900 was powered by a compact, water-cooled, 16-valve four-cylinder engine, which produced 75kw (100bhp), and propelled the Ninja to a then-amazing 240km/h (150mph).

Large sidecars like this Wessex model fitted to a Honda meant a motorcycle could serve as (a rather rudimentary) family transport.

But the GPZ900R also had the handling and braking to match, so much so that it took the first three places in the 1984 production-based Isle of Man TT race.

For the rest of the 1980s, the superbike class developed progressively. Suzuki launched its GSX-R750 race-replica machine in 1985, Honda released its CBR600F and Yamaha's FZR1000 EXUP topped the unlimited-class performance tree in 1989. Japanese engines and horsepower were by now superb: the FZR1000 EXUP produced over 93kw (125bhp) from its 998cc (60ci), 20-valve inline-four water-cooled engine. Attention was now turning to chassis performance and the design of frames, suspension, tyres and brakes to match the sheer motive drive of these engines. French tyre giant Michelin developed the first commercial radial motorcycle road tyre in 1987, and this significantly improved grip, stability and mileage over previous cross-ply designs. Together with stiff, lightweight aluminium frames (first used by Suzuki on its RG250 Gamma), and race-developed suspension and braking systems, the new chassis technologies came together on the FZR1000, allowing the machine's rider to make the most of the engine's power.

By the end of the 1980s, there were signs of a response to the Japanese dominance of the superbike market. Italian firm Ducati began producing a new water-cooled, fuel-injected eight-valve V-twin engine, in a race-replica chassis. The 851, as it was called, may not have been the most auspicious road bike when launched, but it soon began to take victories in the fledgling World Superbike racing championship. Weight and capacity breaks for V-twin engines allowed the 851cc (52ci) Ducati to run with, and beat, the heavier 750cc (46ci) four-cylinder bikes originating from Japan.

Building upon the success of the 851 was the next-generation Ducati twin, the legendary 916 Superbike launched in 1993. Not only did the 916 go on to be the most successful production-based World Superbike racer, but it also brought a new level of automotive styling and exotic design to the world of motorcycling.

Although the Ducati 916 was without question the most desirable motorcycle around when launched, the might of Japan had already moved the game on another step. Launched the previous year, in 1992,

Racing has always improved the motorcycling breed: here, TT winner Alex George leads the pack at Brands Hatch on his Yamaha TZ750.

Honda's CBR900RR FireBlade showed the way forward for superbike design, with its attention to weight loss, chassis dynamics and rider control. Weighing in at just 185kg (408lb) and with a 91kw (122bhp) four-cylinder 16-valve water-cooled engine, the FireBlade was 24kg (53lb) lighter than the FZR1000 EXUP. That reduced weight gave a totally new dimension to the FireBlade's handling and performance. It accelerated, turned and braked much quicker than any other machine. This path was followed by later updates of the FireBlade, with less weight and more power, keeping the CBR900 on top until 1997, when Yamaha launched its YZF-R1, which took a further leap forwards in high power and low weight. The R1 produced 112kw (150bhp) while weighing just 177kg (390lb).

Of course, it was not just pure sporting bikes that were to take great leaps forward in the latter part of the twentieth century. The technology of more powerful, reliable engines and lighter, stronger chassis parts was also incorporated in touring, cruising and off-road machinery. Honda's ST1100 Pan European and VFR800 used the firm's V-four expertise, gained from World Superbike racing, and applied this to both the touring and sports-touring markets. Yamaha built its mighty V-Max, remarkable for both a drag-race styling and explosive power from a 1200cc (73ci) V-four engine.

The 1990s saw the reappearance of some familiar names into mainstream motorcycle production, as well as the emergence of new firms. German firm BMW built on the success of its long-running two-valve Boxer engine with an all-new advanced R1100 four-valve Boxer design, launched in 1993. Together with its horizontal inline-four 'K' series engine, BMW produced a whole new range of sporting, touring and off-road machinery with sound performance and typical BMW values of strong build quality, reliability and tough residuals.

R 1150 RS

In the UK, a new firm backed by property tycoon John Bloor bought the rights to the Triumph marque and began building a range of modern machines in a purpose-built factory in Hinckley, England. And in Italy, Aprilia advanced from producing scooters and small-capacity machines to design and build its own superbike, the RSV1000 Mille. Benelli was also resurrected by Italian millionaire Andrea Merloni and launched its Tornado 900 triple superbike, having built up its finances by selling a range of scooters.

Other Italian firms fared less well: Bimota, Laverda and Moto Guzzi all suffered serious financial problems, resulting in closure. Laverda and Moto Guzzi were bought by Aprilia, Bimota was the subject of various rescue attempts through the early years of the 21st century, and the Rimini firm's future still remains uncertain.

The influence of World Superbike racing on sports motorcycles continued: Ducati's 916 range still dominated, but Honda's 750cc (46ci) RC45 snatched a championship victory in 1997 with US rider John Kocinski. But it had become clear that a 1000cc (61ci) V-twin was the ideal configuration, so both Honda and Suzuki produced such bikes: the VTR1000 and TL1000 ranges. There were race and road-biased versions of both, the VTR1000F Firestorm and VTR1000 SP-1 from Honda and the TL1000S and TL1000R from Suzuki. Only Honda had any real success on track, though: Texan racer Colin Edwards won the WSB championship twice on the Honda SP-1 and SP-2 variant.

In this book, then, we shall explore and explain the technologies and history behind the most important modern superbikes, as well as the experiences provided by these most intensely developed machines.

BMW's R1150RS offers an impressive blend of high-tech performance and comfort. It is one of the best sports-tourers ever produced.

ITALY

Aprilia RS125

Small, but perfectly formed, Aprilia's RS125 is a pocket-sized superbike, with all the styling and performance equipment of its bigger brothers, and superb handling.

The RS125 uses a constant mesh, six-speed gearbox, driven by a multiplate wet clutch, with chain final drive.

Race-type 40mm (1.57in) upside-down front forks have wheel travel of 120mm (4.7in).

A single four-piston caliper operates on a 320mm (12.6in) fully floating stainless steel disc.

The single-cylinder water-cooled two-stroke engine is a strong, reliable design which uses reed-valve crankcase induction and has an electronically operated exhaust power valve. It is also available in an 11kw (15bhp) restricted version for learner riders.

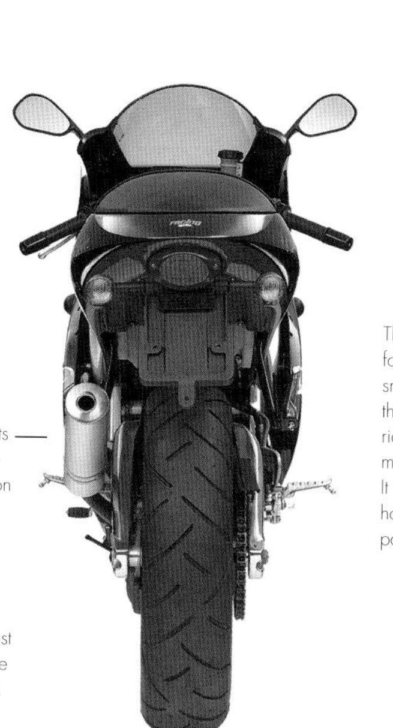

The RS125 benefits from a large, well-designed expansion chamber-type exhaust with a separate silencer. The shape of the chamber reflects pulses in the exhaust gas flow to improve the power delivery.

The moulded plastic fairing ensures a smooth airflow over the machine and rider, increasing maximum speed. It also carries a handsome race-replica paint scheme.

A 125cc (7.6ci) engine is about the minimum required for a true sports bike. It is the smallest capacity class in the Grand Prix class and is where most manufacturers' sports ranges begin. It is also where most novices start out: a 125cc (7.6ci) machine is the biggest that a learner rider can use on the road.

Aprilia's RS125 is one of the most successful and sporty 125s produced. The Italian firm provided the bike with all the traditional components of a true sports

To match the aluminium frame, Aprilia developed an exotic aluminium swingarm, with a braced section on the right and a 'gull-arm' curved section on the left. This curved section allows the exhaust to be tucked out of the way, improving ground clearance.

bike, including a super-stiff, lightweight aluminium twin-beam frame and swingarm, monoshock rear suspension and upside-down front forks. The engine is a typical 125 single-cylinder two-stroke design, but it is an advanced design, with water-cooling and an electronic exhaust port control valve to improve driveability. The bike's ancillary components are also very high quality parts, normally found only on bigger sports machines: four-piston front brake caliper and floating 320mm (12.6in) disc, radial sports tyres with a wide, sticky 150-section rear.

BRILLIANT CORNERING

From the rider's seat, the RS125 makes no secret of its superbike heritage. The riding position is low and sporty, while a race-style dashboard incorporates a clear tachometer and speedometer. High footpegs give good ground clearance for extreme cornering performance, and the aerodynamic full fairing gives the impression of riding a much bigger machine. The performance is remarkable for such a compact bike, the tiny motor producing around 24.6kw (33bhp), enough to propel the RS125 to over 160km/h (100mph). But it is in cornering that the RS125 proves itself. The tiny 115kg (253lb) dry weight, together with the stiff frame and sports tyres, allows the Aprilia to out-perform many larger machines.

Aprilia RS125

Top speed:	147km/h (92mph)
Engine type:	124.8cc (7.6ci), l/c two-stroke single-cylinder
Max power:	24.6kw (33bhp) @ 11,000rpm
Frame type:	twin-spar aluminium
Tyre sizes:	front 110/70 17, rear 150/60 17
Final drive:	chain
Gearbox:	six-speed
Weight:	115kg (253lb)

ITALY

Aprilia RS250

With a short, Grand Prix-inspired chassis, high-revving two-stroke engine and strong power-to-weight ratio, Aprilia's RS250 is the choice for racetrack adrenalin junkies.

In 1998, Aprilia updated the RS250 with a new, more aerodynamic fairing, a revised frame and higher specification suspension components. The bike shown here is one of these later models.

A combination of cast and extruded aluminium parts are welded together to form a curvaceous gull-wing swingarm. The curved side allows the exhaust system to be tucked in, while the braced left-hand side improves stiffness while retaining lightness.

The aerodynamic rear seat unit has a thin pillion pad, which can be removed for solo use.

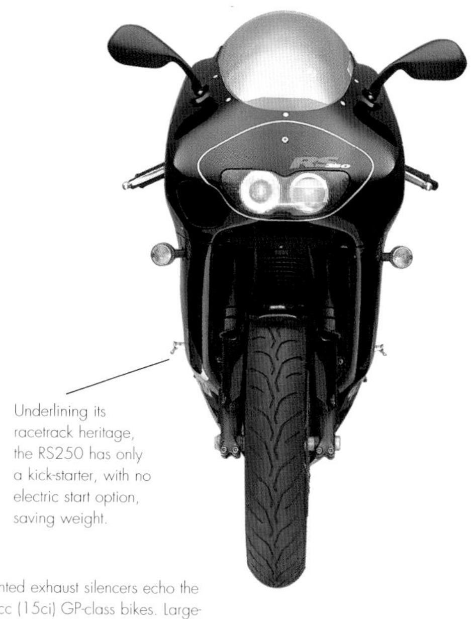

Underlining its racetrack heritage, the RS250 has only a kick-starter, with no electric start option, saving weight.

Twin side-mounted exhaust silencers echo the styling of 250cc (15ci) GP-class bikes. Large-capacity expansion chambers snake below the engine, improving both engine power and cornering ground clearance.

Much of Aprilia's success in Grand Prix racing has come in the 250cc (15ci) class, so it was no surprise when the company announced the launch of a 250cc (15ci) supersports bike in 1994. But few observers expected such a high-specification machine as the RS250, which was powered by a version of Suzuki's RGV250 two-stroke engine because Aprilia's own race powerplant was unsuitable for mass-market production. That engine was the most advanced in its class - a 90 degree water-cooled V-twin with electronic guillotine-type exhaust control valves and

The RS250 is powered by a modified Suzuki RGV250 engine, hidden behind the full race fairing and deep frame rails. Guillotine-type 'power valves' alter the dimensions of the exhaust port according to engine rpm, giving more progressive power delivery.

electronically controlled carburettors. Aprilia modified the exhaust and intake systems of the RGV engine, which produces almost 52kw (70bhp) in this form.

RACING EXCELLENCE

The chassis is equally impressive. A sculpted aluminium twin-beam frame and 'gull-wing' swingarm gives high levels of stiffness, while contributing to the RS250's light 140kg (309lb) weight. Race-specification upside-down front forks and rear monoshock suspension are fully adjustable for road or track use, and deliver excellent performance, particularly on race circuits. Italian firm Brembo supplies the brakes, and the twin front disc set-up offers great stopping power.

Aprilia paid as much attention to the styling of the RS250 as to its engineering. An all-enveloping full fairing improves aerodynamics at speed, while race replica paint schemes echo the looks of the firm's successful Grand Prix machines.

Riding the RS250 is an exhilarating if challenging experience. The engine has a narrow power band, and constant gear changes are required to keep the engine speed within its most powerful range. The RS250's short 1365mm (5.3in) wheelbase and steep steering head angle make it very fast-steering, and it responds sharply to the smallest steering input.

Aprilia RS250

Top speed:	205km/h (128mph)
Engine type:	249cc (15ci), l/c 90° V-twin two-stroke
Max power:	52kw (70bhp) @ 10,500rpm
Frame type:	twin-spar aluminium
Tyre sizes:	front 110/70 17, rear 150/60 17
Final drive:	chain
Gearbox:	six-speed
Weight:	140kg (309lb)

ITALY

Aprilia RSV Mille

With class-leading power and handling, together with unmistakable Italian styling, Aprilia's RSV1000 Mille is a genuine alternative choice for full-bore superbike fans.

Aprilia's radical design aims to combine good high-speed aerodynamic performance with cutting-edge, angular design. The fuel tank is made of high-strength nylon.

There are six gears in the gearbox, and the clutch has a patented pneumatic slipper mechanism, preventing the decelerating engine from locking the rear wheel when entering a corner hard on the brakes.

The RSV's riding position puts the rider high up on top of the machine, giving very good ground clearance. This allows extreme angles of lean when on a race track.

Rider information is viewed on a comprehensive dashboard, which incorporates a lap timer and an adjustable rev-limiter light, as well as the usual functions of speedo, tacho and warning gauges.

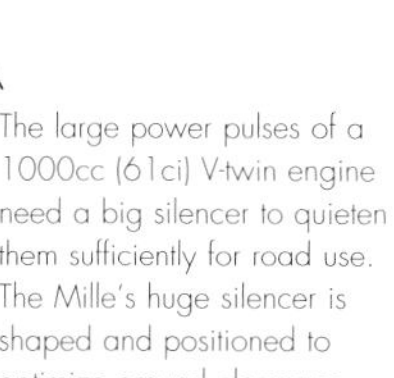

The large power pulses of a 1000cc (61ci) V-twin engine need a big silencer to quieten them sufficiently for road use. The Mille's huge silencer is shaped and positioned to optimize ground clearance.

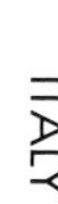

Up until the mid-1990s, there was only really one superbike available from Italy: Ducati's 916. But towards the end of 1997, a new contender appeared. The young firm of Aprilia had made no secret of its plans for a new 1000cc (61ci) sports bike, and many images and design sketches had leaked out to the press over the previous three or four years. Even so, many observers were still surprised by the advanced technology used in the bike when it finally arrived.

Although the fairing is removed, the RSV's engine is still obscured by the frame and the cooling system. Developed with help from UK engine consultants Cosworth, it uses a dry-sump lubrication system and a combined gear/chain valvegear mechanism.

The RSV Mille uses an all-new, water-cooled, 60° V-twin engine, with four valves per cylinder, double overhead camshafts and electronic fuel injection.

An extremely sporty chassis is based around a twin-beam aluminium alloy frame. Rear suspension is a single monoshock design, operated by a cast/extruded aluminium swinging arm, while front suspension is by upside-down forks. The brakes are racing Brembo parts - twin four-piston calipers and 320mm (12.6in) discs at the front and a small single piston caliper at the rear.

RSV VARIANT MODELS

Aprilia has had great success with the RSV, and has produced several variant models, as well as ongoing model updates. The RSV Mille type 'R' features more advanced suspension, made by Swedish suspension firm Ohlins, and lightweight OZ racing wheels. The RSV 'R' is well priced and has sold well for Aprilia, unlike the SP version of the RSV. This limited edition machine was intended to allow homologation of the RSV for World Superbike racing and had an engine with different bore and stroke, as well as a radical racing chassis. However, it was more than twice the price of even an RSV Mille type 'R', so it is no surprise that the RSV Mille SP is rarely seen on the road.

Aprilia RSV Mille

Top speed:	280km/h (175mph)
Engine type:	998cc (61ci), l/c 60° V-twin, eight-valve, DOHC
Max power:	97kw (130bhp) @ 9500rpm
Frame type:	twin-spar aluminium
Tyre sizes:	front 120/70 17, rear 190/50 17
Final drive:	chain
Gearbox:	six-speed
Weight:	187kg (411lb)

Bimota Tesi

Many bike designers over the years have sought to improve on telescopic forked front ends. Perhaps the most exotic of these designs was Bimota's Tesi.

The hub-centre steering is controlled by steel rods, with adjustable spherical joints at each end. These adjustments allow for wear, but also allow quick changes to the entire front-end steering geometry.

The bike's fully enclosing bodywork hides the Tesi's working parts and lends a futuristic air to the machine.

The Tesi was available in two engine capacities: the 851 version used an unchanged version of Ducati's 851cc (52ci) Superbike engine, but a larger capacity 904cc (55ci) version was also available. The 851 version was discontinued after two years.

A comprehensive electronic dashboard used a set of LCD indicators and digital readouts instead of traditional analogue dials.

A kingpin joint inside the front wheel's hub allows the wheel to pivot from side to side, which provides the steering lock. The wheel rotates on large-diameter needle roller bearings surrounding the hub kingpin.

It is fitting that such an innovative design as the Tesi takes its name from the Italian for 'thesis'. Indeed, it was as a university thesis that the Tesi first took form, as part of designer Pierluigi Marconi's degree work. The engineering principles behind the Tesi were fairly simple. Rather than transfer braking, suspension and steering forces through the front forks, the Tesi's swingarm front end separated these forces out. So brake forces were directed through the swingarm directly into the main frame,

The Tesi uses a pair of milled aluminium plates either side of the Ducati engine to mount its front and rear swingarms. Steel-tube subframes support the seat, bodywork and steering gear.

suspension forces were managed by an offset monoshock, and steering is managed by a small pivot inside the front wheel hub. Adjustable rods connected to the steering head operate this pivot.

EXPERIMENTAL PROBLEMS

In practice, however, it took a huge investment in time and research to perfect the system. Initial experiments with hydraulic steering operation ran into serious problems, and the control rod system was eventually adopted. Although the hub steering front end did offer improved characteristics, it was not without its own complications. The Tesi had a cripplingly small steering lock, making slow speed manoeuvring very difficult. The control rods also had to be adjusted from time to time and were susceptible to wear and damage.

The rest of the bike was more conventional - the engine began as an 851 Ducati motor, but was increased in capacity to 904cc (55ci) in 1992 by increasing the stroke to 68mm (2.7in).

The Tesi was not very successful. Its price was too high, and the radical front end did not sufficiently improve handling over conventional telescopic fork systems. In 1993, the Rimini firm produced an 'Edizione Special' with different wheels and cosmetics, but in 1996 the Tesi was discontinued.

Bimota Tesi

Top speed:	249km/h (155mph)
Engine type:	904cc (55ci), l/c 90° V-twin, eight-valve, DOHC desmodromic
Max power:	84kw (113bhp) @ 8500rpm
Frame type:	double aluminium plates
Tyre sizes:	front 120/70 17, rear 180/55 17
Final drive:	chain
Gearbox:	six-speed
Weight:	188kg (414lb)

ITALY

Bimota SB8R

Marrying a superb V-twin engine from Suzuki with an innovative supersport chassis from Bimota, the SB8R is a true thoroughbred superbike.

The SB8R uses carbon-fibre bodywork parts, which combine light weight with great strength. A pair of distinctive air ducts sweep back from the top fairing over the cockpit and back to the fuel tank, feeding the airbox intakes with cool, high-pressure air.

A hydraulic steering damper was fitted to the SB8R to prevent front end instability under hard acceleration.

The main aluminium frame beams are bolted to the extremely rigid, fabricated carbon-fibre swingarm pivot plates.

A separate reservoir of oil and pressurized gas helps prevent the rear shock overheating during hard use.

The twin-beam headlight is the same design as that used on Suzuki's TL1000R.

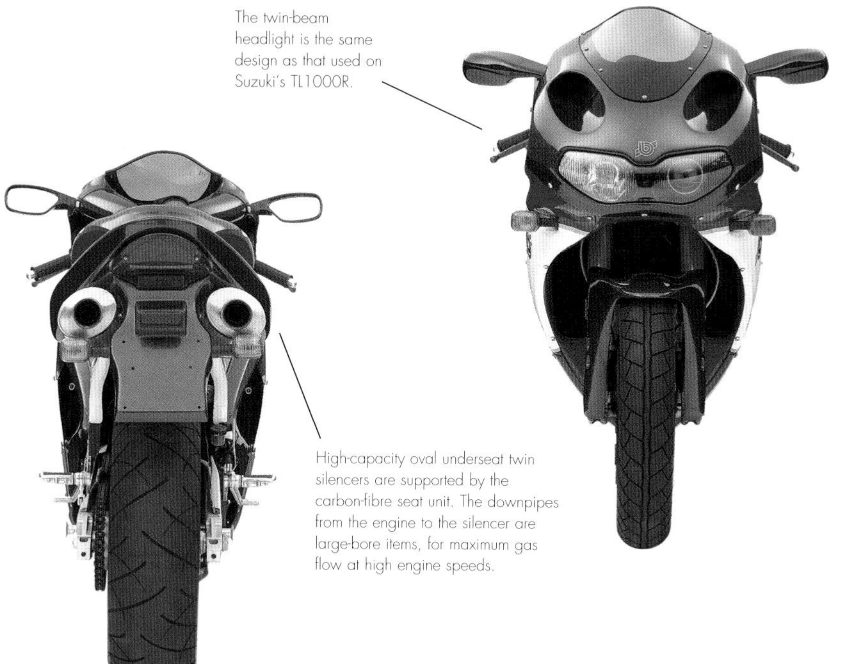

High-capacity oval underseat twin silencers are supported by the carbon-fibre seat unit. The downpipes from the engine to the silencer are large-bore items, for maximum gas flow at high engine speeds.

Italian firm Bimota made its name in the 1970s producing bespoke, performance chassis for the poor-handling but high-powered Japanese machinery of the time. Bikes such as the early SB and KB ranges used advanced materials and design, which, combined with powerful Japanese engines, made for potent sportsbike packages. But by the late 1990s, Japanese chassis technology had caught up with their engines, and mainstream superbikes from Honda, Suzuki, Yamaha and Kawasaki offered handling and braking prowess to match their 97kw (130bhp) power outputs.

Hidden behind fairing panels and the frame, the fully adjustable Paioli rear shock is notable for its off-centre positioning, to allow space for the engine's rear cylinder exhaust exit. It is operated by a linkage and bellcrank.

But the launch of Suzuki's TL1000S and R showed that there was still a space for specially produced performance chassis. The TL1000S was dogged by accusations of poor handling in the press and from owners, and the TLR was heavy and unsophisticated.

STRONG BUT LIGHT

But the TL engine is an excellent performer, and Rimini-based Bimota soon announced plans for a new TL1000R-based bike. When the SB8R was presented in 1999, it was exotic, even for a Bimota. The frame was made from conventional aluminium beams running down from the steering head. But the pivot plates at the swingarm mounting area are made from light, stiff carbon fibre, giving massive strength while being even lighter than a normal aluminium design.

The rest of the chassis is equally impressive: Italian firm Paioli supplied the 46mm (1.8in) upside-down front forks and rear monoshock. Bimota developed its own Marelli fuel injection system and exhaust for the SB8R. The standard Suzuki fuel injection was replaced by massive 59mm (2.3in) throttle bodies, fed by large carbon ram-air intakes from the front fairing. A stainless-steel and aluminium exhaust system further improved peak power and reduced weight over the Suzuki design.

Bimota SB8R

Top speed:	272km/h (170mph)
Engine type:	996cc (61ci), l/c 90° V-twin, eight-valve, DOHC
Max power:	103kw (138bhp) @ 9500rpm
Frame type:	aluminium twin spar/carbon-fibre plates
Tyre sizes:	front 120/70 17, rear 180/55 17
Final drive:	chain
Gearbox:	six-speed
Weight:	178kg (392lb)

BMW R1100S

With a taut, sporty chassis, quirky styling and a strong engine, the R1100S is BMW's best sportsbike and a genuine alternative to other Japanese and European machinery.

Four-piston dual Brembo brake calipers can be fitted with an optional ABS anti-lock braking system for safe stopping on slippery surfaces. Later models also came with 'Evo' electro-hydraulic servo assistance.

Integrated handguard/indicators guide wind and weather past the rider's hands. Optional heated grips improve comfort in cold conditions.

The pillion seat cover is quickly removable to carry a passenger.

The front Telelever suspension system uses hollow telescopic struts to hold the wheel and a wishbone linkage to operate a central monoshock. This gives excellent performance, particularly under braking.

Twin underseat exhausts improve ground clearance and lend a stylish air to the rear end. Catalysts in the system reduce exhaust emissions.

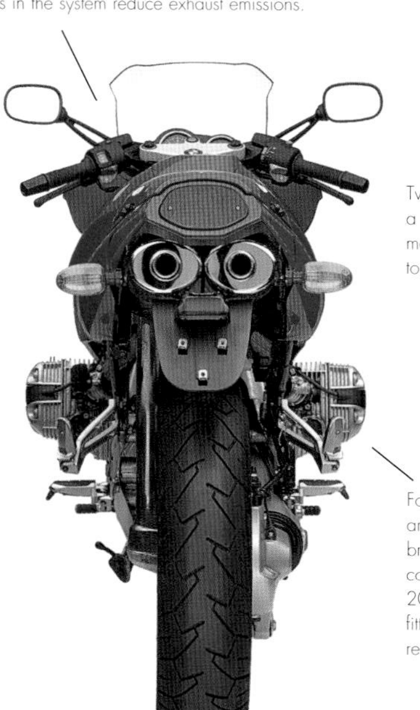

Twin air intakes cool a small oil radiator mounted inside the top fairing.

Four-valve cylinder heads are located in the cooling breeze, helping make water-cooling unnecessary. From 2003, the Boxer engine was fitted with twin spark plugs to reduce emissions.

It is a measure of BMW's particular focus on motorcycle design that its most sporting motorcycle, the R1100S, is matched most evenly to the sports touring class from most other manufacturers. Measured against bikes such as Yamaha's YZF-R1, the R1100S is found wanting, but against a machine such as Triumph's Sprint ST or Honda's VFR800, it is a genuine alternative.

The R1100S is very much a BMW, following the firm's traditional design brief: a flat-twin, air-cooled engine with shaft drive

When the bodywork is removed, the 18l (3.95gal) fuel tank can clearly be seen located under a plastic fairing/ tank cover unit.

and Telelever and Paralever suspension systems. The difference with the S is that all the components have been replaced by more sporting designs, so the engine is an uprated version of that on the R1100 roadster, with 73kw (98bhp) and 9.8kg/m (71lb/ft) of torque. The suspension units front and rear are adjustable, the brakes are twin-disc Brembo parts and the 43cm (17in) aluminium wheels wear sporting radial tyres. There are also various factory sport options available, including a wider rear wheel for more grip.

EASY RIDING

On the road, the R1100S offers a stable, reassuring handling package, with easy, lively drive from the big flat-twin engine. The three-quarter fairing gives protection from windblast, and the dash is simply and clearly laid out. The engine has a broad spread of power, while the six-speed gearbox lets the rider make the most of the power.

Although the R1100S is heavy for a sports bike, this is actually one of BMW's lightest models, and the reduced weight helps braking and handling. Indeed, on a circuit, with sticky race tyres, it is possible for advanced riders to scrape the cylinder head covers during hard cornering – which can be rather disconcerting.

BMW R1100S

Top speed:	224km/h (139mph)
Engine type:	1085cc (66ci), a/c flat-twin, eight-valve, high-cam
Max power:	73kw (98bhp) @ 7500rpm
Frame type:	cast aluminium/steel tube, stressed engine
Tyre sizes:	front 120/70 17, rear 170/60 17
Final drive:	shaft
Gearbox:	six-speed
Weight:	208kg (459lb) [with fuel]

BMW R1150GS

Do not be fooled by the R1150GS's imposing stature and heavyweight off-road looks. It is actually a practical, user-friendly touring machine.

These wire-spoked wheels are a special design, with cross-spoked construction. This allows tubeless tyres to be fitted because the rims are not pierced by the spokes in the centre.

The large 22.1l. (4.9gal) fuel tank allows a considerable range, essential for desert races such as the Paris-Dakar. An optional 30l (6.6gal) tank is also available.

The R1150GS has a touring-friendly six-speed gearbox with overdrive, rather than the five-speed unit of the older R1100GS.

The single-sided rear swingarm incorporates BMW's Paralever shaft drive system, which reduces adverse suspension movement under power. The single-sided arm also allows easy rear wheel removal.

The small, clear windscreen has three adjustable positions to suit different rider heights and can also be removed altogether, if required.

The R1150 engine is oil-cooled, with four-valve 'high-cam' heads. This head design uses camshafts mounted next to the cylinders, with short pushrods operating the valves. This means a more compact head, while allowing high-rpm performance.

BMW has always placed a very high emphasis on the off-road ability of its machinery, none more so than the GS range. 'GS' stands for 'Gelande Strasse', or off-road/road, pointing to the dual nature of the bike's design.

The R1150GS is the pinnacle of BMW's large trailbike design. It is built around the Bavarian firm's trademark flat-twin air-cooled engine, although this latest design uses a high-cam design and fuel injection to improve power and efficiency. The

The front Telelever suspension arm can clearly be seen below the fuel tank, pivoting on the engine casings, with its single shock in the centre.

chassis is equally innovative, using BMW's Telelever suspension at the front and Paralever at the back. Telelever uses a single shock operated by a wishbone and two telescopic sliding struts in an attempt to overcome the inadequacies of traditional telescopic forks, particularly dive under braking. Paralever uses a system of linkages to reduce the effect of the drive shaft on the machine's geometry. Both these systems provide exceptional road-holding and handling for a machine of this size.

POPULAR TOURER

The off-road influence on the design of the R1150GS is clear to see. Wire-spoked wheels wear dirtbike-styled tyres, while a high exhaust and long-travel suspension give exceptional ground clearance.

But while the GS's off-road prowess has been proven by hardened desert racers over the years, it is the bike's usefulness as a touring machine which has cemented its popularity with owners. The soft, long travel suspension gives a comfortable ride, the extended fuel range suits long-distance travel and there is ample pillion provision. Add in a maintenance-free shaft drive and factory optional hard luggage systems, and you see a machine as comfortable crossing Europe as it is racing across Saharan sand dunes.

BMW R1150GS

Top speed:	193km/h (120mph)
Engine type:	1130cc (69ci), a/c flat-twin, eight-valve, high-cam
Max power:	63kw (84bhp) @ 6750rpm
Frame type:	cast aluminium/steel tube, stressed engine
Tyre sizes:	front 110/80 19, rear 150/70 17
Final drive:	shaft
Gearbox:	six-speed
Weight:	228kg (503lb) [with fuel]

GERMANY

BMW K1200LT

With a mission statement to mimic a luxury BMW car on two wheels, BMW's K1200LT is the last word in opulent motorcycle touring.

A powerful four-speaker CD/radio unit is controlled by a tanktop console.

The handlebar switchgear includes stereo, windscreen, heated grips and cruise controls, as well as the normal lighting and control functions.

This small lever engages the electric reversing aid, using the starter motor to help manoeuvre the K1200LT backwards.

The immense seats can be fitted with optional electrical heaters for cold conditions.

The massive luggage space in the rear contains accessories such as a torch, vanity mirror and the optional six-disc CD changer unit.

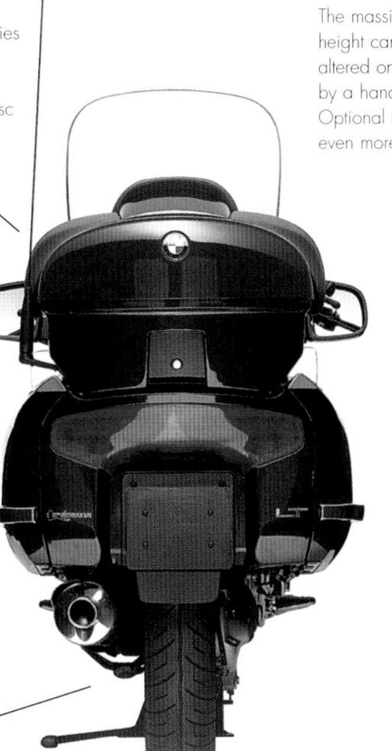

The shaft final drive has a Paralever linkage system to reduce the inertial effect of the shaft under acceleration.

The massive windscreen's height can be electrically altered on the move by a handlebar switch. Optional extensions give even more protection.

Small plastic covers on either side protect the K1200 from most damage in minor slow-speed crashes.

The letters 'LT' here stand for 'Luxury Touring', and this heavyweight tourer certainly lives up to its name. Built to compete head-on with Honda's legendary Gold Wing tourer, the K1200LT is a supremely capable machine, which certainly fulfils its aim of being a two-wheel version of BMW's luxury 7-series car.

The LT is built around a platform of the laid-down 1171cc (71ci) inline-four 'K' series engine. The engine is encased first by a three-part frame, which uses the engine

Even without bodywork, the engine is still hidden. Water-cooled and fuel-injected, the 16-valve DOHC engine produces just under 75kW (100bhp), but with the strong low-rpm torque that is essential for a heavyweight tourer.

cases as load-bearing parts, then in turn by fully enveloping bodywork. This bodywork offers the rider complete protection from windblast and the weather to reduce fatigue on long touring trips.

INTELLIGENT LUXURY

Like the rest of BMW's touring range, the LT uses the firm's patented Telelever and Paralever front and rear suspension systems. These clever designs allow the LT to handle much better than it would with conventional suspension systems, although its sheer mass (345kg/761lb with fuel) and limited ground clearance mean care is needed when riding at high speed. Low-speed riding can also be tricky, until the rider is used to the mass, but a reverse gear does help with parking and other walking-pace manoeuvres. Also of assistance are the integral ABS anti-lock brakes, which make stopping the LT's bulk much more reassuring, particularly on cold or wet road surfaces.

It is, however, the extensive equipment list - standard and optional - which defines the K1200LT experience. From the two-speaker radio system, cavernous hard luggage and ABS through to the trip computer, electrically heated seats and grips, CD changer audio system and satellite navigation of the options list, the LT is an amazingly well-equipped touring motorcycle.

BMW K1200LT

Top speed:	208km/h (130mph)
Engine type:	1171cc (71ci), l/c inline-four, 16-valve, DOHC
Max power:	73kw (98bhp) @ 6750rpm
Frame type:	cast aluminium
Tyre sizes:	front 120/70 17, rear 160/70 17
Final drive:	shaft
Gearbox:	five-speed
Weight:	345kg (759lb) [with fuel]

GERMANY

BMW K1200RS

A true heavyweight sports tourer, BMW's K1200RS is massively powerful, massively fast and massively massive. It is a tool for serious mileage junkies only.

BMW offers a large range of optional accessories for the K1200RS. These include hard luggage systems, a more comfortable seat and heated handlebar grips.

The K1200RS comes with a sophisticated ABS anti-lock braking system and can be specified with cruise control.

Although the 16-valve K1200 engine is a modern unit, it can trace its design roots back to the K100 eight-valve engine of the early 1980s.

The four-into-one exhaust is cunningly designed to fit into the short space between the engine exhaust ports and the silencer. The large-volume muffler has an integral three-way catalyzer unit to reduce emissions.

The dashboard has a simple layout, with analogue dial instruments. Handlebar-mounted mirrors give the rider a good view behind.

BMW's patented Telelever suspension system works at its best on a fast, heavy machine such as this. Its inherent anti-dive characteristics under braking permit much softer suspension settings, improving ride and handling.

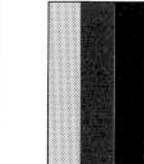

Both the fastest and most powerful machine in BMW's motorcycle range, the K1200RS is aimed at riders who need a fast, comfortable machine to cross large distances. It is powered by a unique 'laid-down' inline-four engine design. This layout turns the engine onto its side and has the crankshaft running along the centreline of the bike, fore and aft. The pistons move back and forth across the bike, and the cylinder head is positioned on the rider's left-hand side.

Located behind bodywork below the seat, the K1200RS's rear monoshock unit is adjustable for spring preload and rebound damping. It is operated by a Paralever linkage swingarm.

Despite its rather eccentric positioning, the engine is a largely conventional design, water-cooled, fuel-injected and with twin overhead camshafts and 16 valves. An electronic fuel injection system is utilized, and the transmission runs through a dry clutch, six gears and a shaft final drive to the rear wheel.

HEAVY WEIGHT

The RS's frame is a composite arrangement, using aluminium castings and steel components, and also using the engine casings as load-bearing members. The suspension front and rear is identifiably BMW - the Telelever front and single-sided Paralever rear allow the rider to get the most from the bike's performance.

The major problem for the K1200RS, though, is its extreme mass. Tipping the scales at 285kg (627lb) fully fuelled, it can be a handful to manoeuvre at slow speeds, and both brakes and engine have to work extra hard to overcome the weight. Conversely, the K1200RS is very stable at speed, helped by conservative steering geometry and its aerodynamic fairing.

Rider comfort is also enhanced by the fairing, as well as a relaxed riding position, and there is a host of official factory options such as heated grips, hard luggage and satellite navigation systems.

BMW K1200RS

Top speed:	256km/h (160mph)
Engine type:	1171cc (71ci), l/c inline-four, 16-valve, DOHC
Max power:	97kw (130bhp) @ 8750rpm
Frame type:	cast aluminium
Tyre sizes:	front 120/70 17, rear 170/60 17
Final drive:	shaft
Gearbox:	five-speed
Weight:	285kg (627lb) [with fuel]

GERMANY

Buell X1 Lightning

Buell's Lightning is an unconventional sports bike. A short wheelbase and centralized mass give nimble handling and get the best from the Harley-Davidson engine.

A small screen deflects wind up and over the rider. The screen unit also holds the analogue speedometer and tachometer.

The complex exhaust system links front and rear downpipes to a large single silencer, mounted below the engine. This layout gives good ground clearance and carries weight lower down, for a lower centre of gravity.

The front brake is an extremely large 340mm (13.4in) single stainless-steel floating disc, operated by an opposed six-piston caliper.

Operated in extension by linkages, the fully adjustable rear shock has been moved below the engine to keep the chassis short and improve rear cylinder exhaust pipe routing.

The Lightning's styling is dominated by the huge side-mounted plastic airbox, essential to get strong power and low noise emissions from the air-cooled OHV engine.

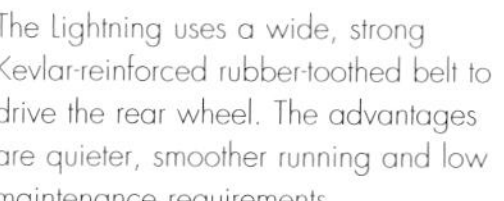

The Lightning uses a wide, strong Kevlar-reinforced rubber-toothed belt to drive the rear wheel. The advantages are quieter, smoother running and low maintenance requirements.

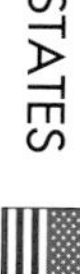

UNITED STATES

By the time the X1 Lightning first appeared in 1999, Buell company founder Erik Buell had been building his range of unique American sports bikes for almost two decades. The former Harley-Davidson engineer began designing his own machines in 1982 with a 750cc (46ci) two-stroke race bike, but his trademark design of a large-capacity V-twin engine in a short, sporty chassis first appeared in 1985.

The X1 Lightning follows typical Buell design principles and includes a very

Snaking below the fuel tank and airbox, the perimeter steel-tube frame offers high torsional stiffness with light weight. The vibrations from the unbalanced engine are absorbed by ingenious flexible mounts.

short wheelbase, light weight and highly centralized mass. Its engine, based on a Harley-Davidson design, uses a 1203cc (74ci) OHV 45 degree V-twin layout. It combines a mix of old and new technologies - carburation is by electronic fuel injection, while valve operation is by old-fashioned pushrods, and cooling is by air. The low-revving engine delivers a strong burst of torque low down in the rev range, although the power tails off quickly. The power is transmitted to the rear wheel through a five speed gearbox and a tough, low-maintenance aramid/rubber final drive belt.

UNIQUE RIDING

Buell's offbeat design mix extends to the chassis. A perimeter steel-tube frame is very stiff and light, and the front forks are fully adjustable Japanese Showa parts. The rear shock is also a Showa, but is mounted in an unusual underslung configuration, further lowering the centre of gravity.

The Buell's riding experience is also unique. The rider sits in an aggressive, upright position, providing complete control. The centralized mass, short wheelbase and steep steering geometry make for a quick-steering chassis. This sharp, taut handling is thrown into contrast, however, by the low-revving and rather harsh engine.

Buell X1 Lightning

Top speed:	200km/h (125mph)
Engine type:	1203cc (74ci), a/c 45° V-twin, four-valve, OHV
Max power:	75kw (101hp) @ 6000rpm
Frame type:	Chrome-moly steel tube perimeter
Tyre sizes:	front 120/70 17, rear 170/60 17
Final drive:	Kevlar belt
Gearbox:	five-speed
Weight:	200kg (440lb)

ITALY

Cagiva Raptor

Designed by the man who created Ducati's Monster, the Cagiva Raptor is a high-performance city roadster, with Japanese power courtesy of a Suzuki TL1000S engine.

The Raptor has a steep steering head angle, which allows quick turning. But this can lead to instability over bumpy surfaces, and many owners fit a steering damper.

Cagiva also produced a V-Raptor, with a small nose cone and lower handlebars.

The Raptor has a single-piece dual seat for rider and pillion. It comes with a plastic rear seat cover, for use when there is no passenger.

The front Brembo brakes use dual four-piston calipers. Braided steel hoses give a firm feel at the lever and strong stopping power.

The rear double-sided swingarm is made from extruded aluminium. It operates an adjustable rear monoshock.

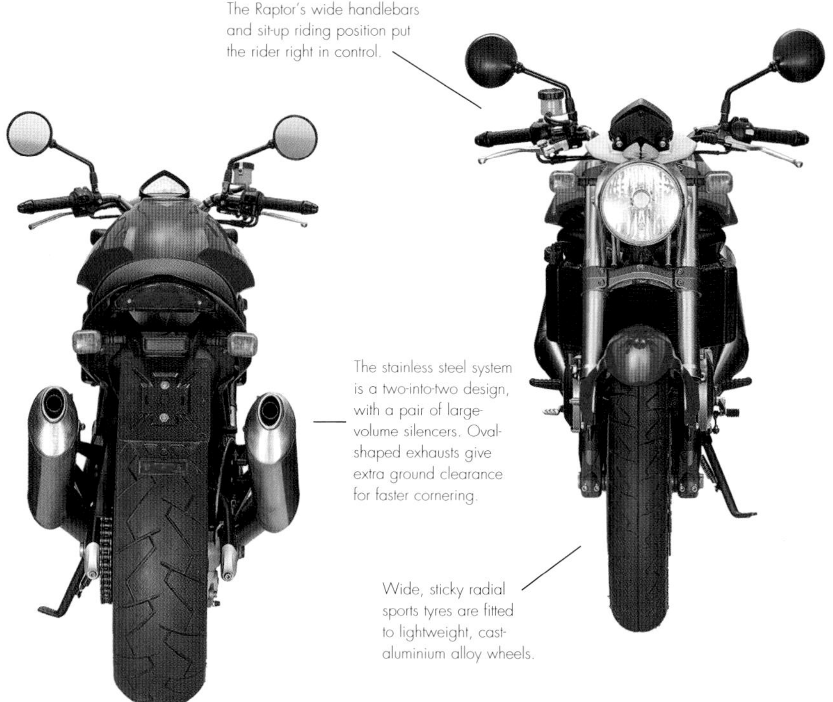

The Raptor's wide handlebars and sit-up riding position put the rider right in control.

The stainless steel system is a two-into-two design, with a pair of large-volume silencers. Oval-shaped exhausts give extra ground clearance for faster cornering.

Wide, sticky radial sports tyres are fitted to lightweight, cast-aluminium alloy wheels.

Cagiva's Raptor is a machine which combines the best of both worlds: Italian flair in chassis design and styling, and Japanese efficiency in a reliable, powerful engine. It was designed as a competitor to Ducati's Monster range and, ironically, designed by the man who dreamt up the original Monster, Miguel Galluzzi. Mating a bought-in version of Suzuki's TL1000S engine with a steel-tube trellis- framed chassis, the Raptor proved an excellent package when launched in early 2000. Cagiva's taut, sharp-steering chassis offered sportsbike-like handling, thanks to upside-down front forks, single rear monoshock and high-performance Brembo

Stripped down, the minimalistic steel tube trellis frame of the Raptor can be seen. It is much stiffer than it looks.

brakes. The chassis also features radical design elements, with angular footrest hangers, sharp-edged bodywork and, in the V-Raptor variant, an aggressive nose cone. Even the dashboard dares to be different, with a triangular-shaped tachometer and a LCD speedometer.

CITY SLICKER

The Raptor's water-cooled, eight-valve 90°V-twin engine is a re-badged TL1000S item, with Cagiva's own fuel injection and exhaust systems. These modifications, together with a revised final gear ratio, give the Raptor exceptional performance, with aggressive acceleration in all gears.

Like its distant cousin, the Monster, the Raptor is an unashamed city bike. Extremely popular in Europe, these machines are bought with almost as much emphasis on their styling as on their performance. Galluzzi's combination of daring design with sound, classic motorcycle elements makes the Raptor a clear contender in these terms, as well as a sound performer.

The Raptor's success encouraged Cagiva to launch a smaller 650cc (40ci) version, fitted with a Suzuki SV650 engine. But cashflow problems struck the Varese-based factory in 2002, cutting production of the entire Raptor range and making the striking city bike a rare sight on the road.

Cagiva Raptor

Top speed:	237km/h (147mph)
Engine type:	996cc (61ci), l/c 90° V-twin, eight-valve, DOHC
Max power:	79kw (106bhp) @ 8500rpm
Frame type:	steel-tube trellis
Tyre sizes:	front 120/70 17, rear 180/55 17
Final drive:	chain
Gearbox:	six-speed
Weight:	192kg (423lb)

Ducati 748R

Ducati's middleweight twin is essentially a smaller capacity version of the 916 Superbike. But this exotic, high-specification 'R' version packs a mighty racetrack punch.

Inside the vast 14l (3gal) airbox, an advanced fuel injection system features Formula One-type 'shower' fuel injectors, which point straight into the large 54mm (2.1in) throttle bodies.

A single seat unit and no pillion footrests confirm the 748R as a machine for solo pleasures only.

The gold-coloured titanium nitride coating on the Showa front fork stanchions reduces static friction or 'stiction'. This improves finesse and feel from the fully adjustable suspension components.

A large capacity water radiator and smaller oil cooler help keep the engine's temperature down, even under extreme racetrack conditions.

A large battery is needed to operate the powerful starter motor necessary to turn over the large, high-compression pistons inside the engine. It is mounted behind the side fairing to help centralize the 748R's mass.

Track compound Pirelli Dragon tyres give superlative grip on race tracks and roads alike.

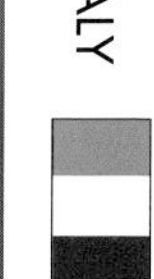

Beginning with this model in 1999, Ducati used the suffix 'R' to denote track-biased variants of its superbike range. Formerly called SPS (sport production special) models, these high-specification track-ready versions had more powerful engines, more advanced suspension and brakes, and lightweight wheels and carbon-fibre fairing components. They also met the requirements of some racing classes, notably World Supersport and World Superbike, for road-going homologation versions of the race bikes to be sold to the public.

The 748R thus followed the familiar pattern of the 748SPS it succeeded. The basic 748cc (46ci), water-cooled, desmodromic,

The trademark Ducati steel-tube trellis frame seen here is incredibly stiff and includes an adjustable steering head. Eccentric clamps allow the rake or castor angle to be varied according to the required setup, to alter the rate of steering.

90° V-twin of the standard 748 received larger valves and more radical camshafts, as well as the stronger titanium conrods of the old SPS. New throttle bodies were fitted to a new, larger airbox, made possible by a revised, 996 racer-based steel tube frame.

RACING PERFORMANCE

The new frame of the Ducati 748R was complemented by a race-specification suspension package: Ohlins rear shock and titanium-nitride-coated Showa front forks, as well as lightweight Marchesini wheels wearing sticky Pirelli tyres. These advanced components reduced the bike's unsprung weight and provided superlative suspension performance. The by-then traditional 916-derived styling was tweaked slightly on the 748R, but the model nevertheless remained recognizable as Ducati's superbike.

Although tiding a 748R on the road is satisfying, it is almost a waste to use such thoroughbred performance on public highways. When Ducati's exotic middle-weight superbike is kept to the racetrack, it provides one of the finest circuit motorcycling experiences available. The suspension, frame, wheels and tyres give extreme handling finesse, while the highly tuned V-twin engine gives its best when used in full-on track mode: revs screaming high, throttle grip twisted wide open.

Ducati 748R

Top speed:	254km/h (158mph)
Engine type:	748cc (46ci), l/c 90° V-twin, eight-valve, DOHC desmodromic
Max power:	79kw (106bhp) @11,500rpm
Frame type:	steel-tube trellis
Tyre sizes:	front 120/60 17, rear 180/55 17
Final drive:	chain
Gearbox:	six-speed
Weight:	192kg (423lb)

Ducati 851

The ancestor of the massively successful 916 range, Ducati's 851 Superbike brought water-cooled desmoquattro power to the racetrack, in a classic, winning package.

The aluminium fuel tank holds 20l (4.4gal). Later fuel tanks were steel.

The 851 used a Weber Marelli fuel injection system, based on a system used on the Ferrari F40 and Ford Sierra RS Cosworth sportscars, among other cars.

The 851 engine was developed from a 748cc (46ci) design, built by Ducati engineer Massimo Bordi. Bordi had championed the idea of a four-valve, desmodromic cylinder head since his days at university, and the engine also featured belt-driven double overhead cams, fuel injection and water-cooling.

A desmodromic valve system uses a camshaft to positively close as well as open the engine's poppet inlet and exhaust valves. This positive closing system, rather than using return springs, allows more radical valve movements and perfect valve control at high engine speeds.

An extruded aluminium swingarm pivots on the rear of the engine's crankcases.

The front forks are upside-down Showa parts. Earlier models used Marzocchi forks.

It was with the 851 that the roots of Ducati's incredible success throughout last decade of the twentieth century lay. First conceived in the mid-1980s by Ducati engineer Massimo Bordi, it was an answer to the impending obsolescence of the air-cooled, two-valve engines then used by Ducati. A new, advanced engine design was needed, and Bordi provided the answer.

The 851 engine first ran on a test bench as a 748cc (46ci), but was soon increased in capacity to 851cc (52ci). It featured a

Stripped down, air intakes can be seen either side of the headlight. These direct cool air onto the cylinder head area, helping power production. The trellis frame and large battery are also visible.

cylinder head designed with help from UK firm Cosworth, four valves per cylinder, electronic fuel injection and liquid-cooling. Ducati's trademark desmodromic valve actuation was also used, ensuring valve control at high engine speeds. This revolutionary engine was fitted to a steel-tube trellis frame with race-specification chassis components: Marvic wheels, Marzocchi suspension, Brembo brakes. The first 851 Strada models produced in late 1987 and 1988 suffered from poor handling, but later models were improved by fitting 43cm (17in) wheels and even better quality suspension. In 1992, Ducati switched to Japanese Showa suspension for the standard 851. The rather boxy bodywork, with its square headlight, quickly dated, but was at the cutting edge of design in the late 1980s.

INCREASED CAPACITY

The 851 gained a capacity increase to 888cc (54ci) in 1992, and the name was also changed to 888. Somewhat confusingly, the SP (Sport Production) version of the 851 produced from 1990 to 1994 also used an 888cc (54ci) engine.

By 1993, the 851's engine had increased in capacity again, this time to 916cc (56ci). This larger engine powered the 916 Superbike and propelled Ducati to almost a decade of success on track and in the showroom.

Ducati 851

Top speed:	240km/h (149mph)
Engine type:	851cc (52ci), l/c 90° V-twin, eight-valve, DOHC desmodromic
Max power:	78kw (105bhp) @ 9000rpm
Frame type:	steel-tube trellis
Tyre sizes:	front 120/70 17, rear 180/55 17
Final drive:	chain
Gearbox:	six-speed
Weight:	180kg (397lb)

ITALY

Ducati 900SS

'SS' stands for 'Super Sport', and it is one of Ducati's oldest, most successful model ranges. The latest 900SS marries this heritage with modern motorcycle design and technology.

The 900SS was also available in a half-faired Sport version, with the bodywork coming to a halt just below the black air intakes.

The shapely steel fuel tank holds 18l (3.96gal) of petrol.

Ducati produced 750 and 600 versions of the SS, with smaller capacity engines. The year 2003 saw an overhaul for the range, with 1000, 800 and 620 capacity engines.

Ducati fitted the 1998 SS with clocks from the 916 Superbike. They are basic analogue dials with speedometer, tachometer and oil temperature gauge.

The 900SS's Showa upside-down front forks are updates borrowed from the ST2, and the rear shock was lengthened for a better damping action over the old design.

The 900SS engine is air- and oil-cooled. Ducts in the fairing help channel cooling airflow to the rear cylinder, and a light aluminium oil radiator in front of the engine further helps temperature control.

Of all Ducati's modern roadbike designs, the SS range is the longest running, dating back to the 750 Super Sport of the early 1970s. And while the latest versions of the SS are modern, fully developed sports bikes, the roots of the design show in the basic design: an air-cooled, four-valve, desmodromic, 90° V-twin engine in a steel-tube trellis chassis.

The 900SS first appeared in 1975, but the last version was first unveiled in 1998. It was a complete model update over the previous version, with many significant design changes. The bodywork was the brainchild

A double-sided braced aluminium swingarm operates the rear monoshock via a simple cantilever linkage, and pivots on the rear of the engine cases.

of Ducati design chief Pierre Terblanche and combined distinctive, attractive, modern styling with good aerodynamic performance. Behind the stylish plastic panels, the venerable SS engine had been heavily revised. Major changes centred on the carburation, the previous Mikuni carburettors having been replaced by a Weber-Marelli fuel injection system, but the engine also had new camshafts, pistons, cylinders and other components aimed at increasing power and reliability.

TRADITIONS CONTINUED

The basic layout of the chassis remained similar to the previous model, to cut costs, but the frame was slightly modified, altering the steering angle. Chassis components came from other models in the Ducati line-up, including the ST2 sports tourer and the 916 superbike.

The end result was a machine firmly in the SS tradition. The two-valve engine produces satisfying power, starting from down low in the rev range through to a strong midrange. Although short on top-end power, its 60kw (80bhp) is sufficient for around 225km/h (140mph).

That said, the SS was always more concerned about blending easy engine performance with connoisseur's handling, in a stylish yet practical roadbike package.

Ducati 900SS

Top speed:	225km/h (140mph)
Engine type:	904cc (55ci), a/c 90° V-twin, four-valve, SOHC desmodromic
Max power:	60kw (80bhp) @ 7500rpm
Frame type:	steel-tube trellis
Tyre sizes:	front 120/70 17, rear 170/60 17
Final drive:	chain
Gearbox:	six-speed
Weight:	188kg (414lb)

Ducati 916

Often described as the 'two-wheeled Ferrari', Ducati's 916 superbike combines gorgeous aesthetic design with superlative handling and performance.

The 916 was designed with an hydraulic steering damper fitted transversely between the steering yokes and the fuel tank.

The 916 originally appeared with a single seat unit. A Biposto (dual seat) model followed one year later, in 1995.

The 916 was built for World Superbike competition, which it dominated totally. The 916 won its inaugural season in 1994, winning again (in various capacities) in 1995, 1996, 1998, 1999 and 2001.

The final-drive chain tension is adjusted by rotating the eccentric rear-axle mount.

The dual headlights are mounted in an innovative cast-aluminium bracket, which also holds the front fairing and instrument panel in place.

Ducts below the headlights feed cool high-pressure air to a sealed ram-airbox.

Despite its high specification, the 916 is unreliable compared with Japanese motorcycles. Electrical and mechanical problems were common with early models, although quality improved steadily throughout the model life.

If Honda's CBR900RR FireBlade defined mainstream, high-performance Japanese sporting motorcycles of the early 1990s, Ducati's 916 did the same job for exotic, esoteric designer superbikes. With its development roots buried deep in the V-twin 851-series racers of the late 1980s and early 1990s, the 916 enthralled the entire motorcycling community at its launch in 1993. It was not just the intriguing beauty of the machine that appealed: more impressive still was the fact that here, in such a stunning package, was an advanced, focused sporting machine.

The 916 engine requires a skilled technician for correct adjustment of its desmodromic valvegear. The camshaft belts also require regular replacement, and servicing costs are higher than less exotic competitors.

RADICAL CHIC

The 916 was designed by master bike designer Massimo Tamburini, who later went on to design the MV Agusta F4, another beautiful, radical machine. Tamburini developed the 916 on the foundations that were laid in the 851 range: a steel-tube trellis frame housing a water-cooled, desmodromi, eight-valve, 90° V-twin engine, with fuel injection. The 916 went much further than the 851, however, in terms of chassis development, integrated design and attention to detail. It abounds with exquisite flourishes - some of them purely cosmetic, such as the double ellipsoidal headlights; some of them functional, such as the side-mounted battery under the fairing. But the design's genius showed in the parts which not only look beautiful, but also fulfil an important engineering role. The curvaceous, cast-aluminium single-sided rear swingarm is a piece of automotive art, but was intended to allow quick wheel changes in endurance racing. And the underseat exhausts provide an unforgettable rear profile, while also improving aerodynamic performance.

The riding experience of the new bike was also unforgettable: the new engine gave strong, linear power delivery, matched to the stable yet dynamic chassis. The 916 was to provide a foundation for Ducati's Superbike racing success throughout the 1990s.

Ducati 916

Top speed:	261km/h (162mph)
Engine type:	916cc (56ci), l/c 90° V-twin, eight-valve, DOHC desmodromic
Max power:	78kw (105bhp) @ 9000rpm
Frame type:	steel-tube trellis
Tyre sizes:	front 120/70 17, rear 190/50 17
Final drive:	chain
Gearbox:	six-speed
Weight:	203kg (448lb)

Ducati 996

Ducati's 916 was still at the top of the class for style in 1998. But competition forced Ducati to boost its performance and capacity, resulting in the 996.

The classic 916 styling was updated, with new, modern logos and a gently restyled fairing.

Increased investment from an American finance group, TGP, improved build quality and reliability. The 996 suffered fewer mechanical problems than the 916.

Early 996s retained the three-spoke Marchesini wheel design of the 916, although they were a lighter design. From 2000, new five-spoke wheels were fitted.

A new alternator and lighting circuit was designed to power both headlights at once on low beam. The 916 only had one beam lit on dip.

From 2000, there were three versions of the 996: a basic Biposto, the 996S with Ohlins suspension and the SPS engine, and the 996R. This was a range-topping machine, with a new 998cc (61ci) engine and other refinements.

Ducati's 916 Superbike was a great success for the Bologna company, but by 1997, competition from Honda's Firestorm, Suzuki's TL1000S and Aprilia's RSV Mille prompted an overhaul. The resulting bike, the 996, had more power, better refinement and improved brakes when it appeared in late 1998.

The name change correlates with a capacity change from 916cc (56ci) to 996cc (61ci). This was a fairly straightforward job, as the special 916SPS had been a 996cc design since 1997. The 996 incorporated the larger 98mm (3.9in) pistons, larger valves, stronger crankshaft and crankcases of the SPS engine, but with 916 camshafts, which

The 996 was the last incarnation of the 916-based engine. From 2001, Ducati's flagship superbike was the 998, which used the Testastretta engine first used on the 996R. This engine had a shorter stroke, new cylinder head design and much higher power potential.

gave a softer, less peaky power delivery and less top-end power: 83.5kw (112bhp) as against the SPS engine's 92.4kw (124bhp). The intake system was redesigned, with twin fuel injectors for each cylinder, and a new airbox, while the distinctive underseat exhaust system was also new.

COMPETITIVE IMPROVEMENTS

Chassis modifications for the 996 were less comprehensive - the 916's handling was already excellent. Wheels were updated with slightly lighter components, and both front and rear brakes overhauled with more powerful calipers, discs and pads. Front forks remained Showa, as did the rear shock, both fully adjustable for damping and preload.

On the road, the 996 was enough of an improvement to match its rivals. While still down on outright power compared with the Firestorm and TL1000S, the 996 remained an unbeatable combination of track handling and evocative styling.

Minor updates in 2000 saw the 996 equipped with new Marchesini wheels and titanium nitride-coated front fork tubes, while an overhaul of the 996 range in 2001 resulted in an Ohlins rear shock for the base 996 model.

The classic 916 styling was also slightly updated, with new, modern logos and a gently restyled fairing.

Ducati 996

Top speed:	266km/h (165mph)
Engine type:	996cc (61ci), l/c 90° V-twin, eight-valve, DOHC desmodromic
Max power:	83.5kw (112bhp) @ 8500rpm
Frame type:	steel-tube trellis
Tyre sizes:	front 120/70 17, rear 190/50 17
Final drive:	chain
Gearbox:	six-speed
Weight:	198kg (437lb)

Ducati 996SPS

Ducati's range-topping flagship sports bike from 1998–2000, the 996SPS is one of the most highly developed race replica machines ever produced.

The distinctive gold-piped white race number panel on the single seat unit immediately marks this machine as an exotic SPS model.

The final SPS of 2000 was 3kg (7lb) lighter than the original, due to the lighter battery, wheels and rear subframe.

Troy Bayliss won the 2001 World Superbike championship on a factory-supported 996R, the 2001 model year successor to the 996SPS.

Both the fully adjustable rear monoshock and the steering damper are high-quality parts by Swedish manufacturer Ohlins.

The Ohlins forks shown here were fitted for the 2000-model bike. Their inner stanchion tubes are coated in gold-coloured titanium nitride, a hard, slippery substance that reduces friction in the forks, improving their operation.

Up until 2000, Ducati sidestands were self-retracting, which caught out many riders, who dropped their machines when the stand sprung up. From 2000, Ducati fitted normal stands to all its bikes.

The 'SPS' suffix to the 996 model name stands for 'Sport Production Special' and denotes a very high specification variant of the standard Ducati 996 machine. Launched in 1998 as a replacement to the 916SPS model (which, confusingly, used a 996cc/61ci engine), the Ducati 996SPS featured higher specification engine and chassis components than those which were used on the standard 996.

The engine was the same as used in the 916SPS, including that bike's titanium conrods and 50mm (1.97in) header pipes in the exhaust system. Producing around 9kw (12bhp) more than the standard 996, the SPS engine was a much stronger track engine,

In 2000, the smaller, maintenance-free battery shown here replaced the heavier unsealed battery used on previous models, saving over 1kg (2.2lb). The air intakes and airbox can also be seen.

with a correspondingly peakier power delivery, more suited to circuit riding.

To ensure a suitable distance remained between the specification of the SPS and the standard bike, the 996SPS enjoyed a more lavish chassis specification. The wheels were five-spoke Marchesinis, lighter than the standard three-spoke designs, and the rear monoshock and steering damper were high-quality adjustable items by Swedish firm Ohlins. Even the standard 996 was an extremely fine-handling machine, so the SPS was among the best performing chassis on the road. An adjustable steering head allowed geometry changes to suit individual riding styles and different race tracks.

RACING SUCCESS

As with the 916SPS, Ducati produced a limited edition 'Foggy Replica' 996SPS to celebrate the success of its WSB rider, Carl Fogarty. Featuring a race-replica paint scheme, 150 bikes were produced in 1999.

Over the two years of its model life, the Ducati 996SPS was steadily updated with more advanced chassis parts, in particular Ohlins front forks, featuring titanium nitride coated fork tubes. An aluminium rear subframe and other detail modifications reduced the motorcycle's weight, further refining what was the already superlative handling package of the 996SPS.

Ducati 996SPS

Top speed:	280km/h (175mph)
Engine type:	996cc (61ci), l/c 90° V-twin, eight-valve, DOHC desmodromic
Max power:	92kw (123bhp) @ 9800rpm
Frame type:	steel-tube trellis
Tyre sizes:	front 120/70 17, rear 190/50 17
Final drive:	chain
Gearbox:	six-speed
Weight:	190kg (418lb)

UNITED STATES

Harley-Davidson Dyna Super Glide Sport

A sporting Harley-Davidson is unlike any other firm's sports bike. The Dyna Super Glide Sport offers an extra dose of performance, while remaining unmistakably Harley.

The single piston front brake calipers shown on this 1999 bike were later replaced by much better four-piston calipers from 2000 onwards. Discs are 292mm (11.5in) in diameter.

The FXDX is fitted with various sporting improvements: its instruments include a tachometer, and the footpegs are rear-mounted, rather than set forward for cruising.

Passengers sit on a separate pad, which can be removed for solo riding. Note passenger footpegs, still fitted to this bike.

The standard exhaust system is too quiet and restrictive for many owners, and aftermarket systems such as this one are often fitted to improve power and give a louder sound.

Early models such as this one used wire-spoked wheels, but cast parts became standard in 2000. Wire-spoked wheels remained available as a factory option.

Perhaps the best known motorcycle manufacturer in the world, Harley-Davidson has pinned its success more on heritage than technological progress. So while other firms sell their sporting models on the back of ever increasing complexity and performance, Harley's sporting range takes a different path. The Dyna Super Glide Sport, like almost every other Harley, is based around the firm's 45° V-twin air-cooled OHV engine. This torquey, low-revving engine is rubber-mounted in a Dyna frame, again a trademark Harley steel-tube design. What differentiates the Superglide

The FXDX uses Harley's most recent air-cooled engine design, the 1449cc (88ci) Twin Cam 88, the '88' referring to the engine's capacity in cubic inches. The design is old-fashioned: the two valves per cylinder are operated by pushrods from two camshafts mounted just above the crankshaft.

from other bikes in the Dyna range is its extra sporting equipment. The forks are modern, fully adjustable cartridge-damped types, rather than old damper-rod designs, while the front brake has twin discs, rather than the single unit on the basic Superglide. The twin rear shocks are also adjustable for preload and rebound damping.

IMPROVED PERFORMANCE

Riding the Super Glide Sport hard is certainly more rewarding than most Harleys. There is sufficient ground clearance for fast cornering, while the twin brake discs give reasonable stopping power, and the suspension offers adequate damping.

This, however, is in comparison to the rather dismal sporting performance of most other Harley-Davidsons: the Superglide Sport has less performance than a Japanese sports bike, with one-third of the capacity. Peak power of 51kw (68bhp) and a 300kg (661lb) dry mass makes for leisurely acceleration and a top speed not much over 160km/h (100mph).

However, pure performance is not Harley's area of interest. Rather, bikes such as the Super Glide Sport are designed to retain the romance and tradition of a Harley-Davidson in a relaxed cruising package, while offering a more dynamic performance potential.

Harley-Davidson Dyna Super Glide Sport

Top speed:	177km/h (110mph)
Engine type:	1449cc (88ci), a/c 45° V-twin, four-valve, OHV
Max power:	51kw (68bhp) @ 5400rpm
Frame type:	steel-tube backbone
Tyre sizes:	front 100/90 19, rear 150/80 16
Final drive:	belt
Gearbox:	five-speed
Weight:	300kg (661lb)

JAPAN

Honda VFR400R NC30

With a compact, race-developed V-four engine and a stiff, lightweight chassis, the VFR400R NC30 is one of the most exotic lightweight sports bikes around.

Japanese home-market NC30s were fitted with a speed-limiting device which prevented speeds above 180km/h (112mph). These devices are commonly disabled by owners.

The small fuel tank holds 15l (3.3 gal) of unleaded petrol.

The seat is very low, making the NC30 ideal for shorter riders.

The design for Honda's single-sided rear suspension arms was partly developed from the pioneering work of the French Elf firm.

The high-mounted stainless-steel silencer exits on the left-hand side of the bike, to allow easy access to the single-sided rear wheel. This is partly for racing use, partly for styling reasons.

The small dual headlights are a similar design to that used on Honda's legendary endurance racers and the 750cc (46ci) RC30 superbike.

The NC30 uses a 46cm (18in) rear wheel, which is not a modern size. Some owners swap this for a 43cm (17in) part, to improve tyre choice.

Restrictions in Japan's licensing laws until the late 1990s meant that 400cc (24ci) machines were the largest capacity bikes most Japanese riders were allowed to own. To ride a larger bike meant passing an incredibly difficult test, and as a result the Japanese market for smaller capacity versions of mainstream sports bikes was a vast one.

Honda's VFR400R NC30 is a typical example of this 400cc (24ci) supersport class, which first appeared in 1989, replacing the earlier NC24 version of the VFR400R. Outwardly similar to the firm's legendary

The VFR's V-four engine is compact and powerful for its capacity. Its four camshafts are driven by gears from the crankshaft, which improves valve timing accuracy and reliability.

VFR750R RC30, the little NC30 is well equipped, with all the high-specification engine and chassis parts of its bigger brother.

Like the RC30, the NC30 uses a compact, reliable V-four four-stroke engine, with exotic gear-driven camshafts. Producing around 48kw (65bhp), the little engine gives the lightweight race-bred chassis great performance, approaching that of contemporary 600cc (37ci) machines.

DISTINCTIVE PROFILE

That chassis had a stiff, light aluminium twin-beam frame as its foundation and also featured an incredibly exotic single-sided rear swingarm. This stylish design, borrowed straight from the glamorous world of endurance racing, gave the little VFR an unmistakable profile and also accentuated the familial resemblance to the bigger RC30. Front forks are conventional designs, and a pair of four-piston brake calipers provides strong stopping power.

First impressions when sitting upon the NC30 are of a tiny machine, with a spartan, racing cockpit. The riding position is racy and places the rider in control over the front end of the bike. At its best on a race track or twisting back roads, the NC30's brakes and suspension work well, although larger riders may overwhelm the chassis, designed as it was for a smaller, Japanese rider.

Honda VFR400R NC30

Top speed:	216km/h (135mph)
Engine type:	399cc (24ci), l/c 90° V-four, 16-valve, DOHC
Max power:	48kw (65bhp) @ 13,000rpm
Frame type:	aluminium twin spar
Tyre sizes:	front 120/60 17, rear 150/60 18
Final drive:	chain
Gearbox:	six-speed
Weight:	164kg (362lb)

JAPAN

Honda CB400 Four Supersport

With all the appeal of Honda's full-bore superbikes, in a small, nimble package, the CB400 Four Supersport was the definitive lightweight sportster of the 1970s.

The single front disc brake is a rather primitive design, and performance in wet weather can be poor. Modern brake pads, however, improve the situation.

The CB400 has a 14l (3.1gal) fuel tank, with a reserve tap.

The CB400 used small 21mm (0.8in) Keihin slide-type carburettors to provide the petrol/air mixture to the engine.

Unlike most modern sports bikes, the CB400 Four is fitted with both centre and kick stands, making basic chain and wheel maintenance much simpler.

The CB400's screw and locknut valve tappets and points ignition mean regular maintenance is essential to keep the engine at peak efficiency.

The exhaust, mudguards, chainguards and other parts were produced from mild steel finished in chrome plate. These parts quickly rusted if not looked after in wet climates and often need replacing during restoration projects.

In the late 1970s, when the CB400 Four was launched, most of the Japanese performance roadsters had a similar layout. This design was based around an air-cooled, four-cylinder engine, mounted transversely in a steel-tube cradle frame, with front disc brakes, rear drum brake, conventional forks and twin rear shocks.

So when Honda presented the CB400 for 1974, there was little in the base specification to catch the eye. The CB400's four-cylinder engine was developed from the

A SOHC, eight-valve air-cooled design was typical Japanese technology of the time. The lightweight valve train and race-developed internal design allowed a high maximum rev ceiling. The kickstart was provided to reassure riders unused to an electric start.

lacklustre CB350 SOHC design, increased in capacity to 408cc (25ci), and with a peppy 28kw (37bhp) output. Together with the lightweight, capable chassis, the engine gave the CB400 a very decent performance package for its time. Even more than two decades on, the 400 Four is still a pleasure to ride on twisty back roads, particularly if it has been slightly modified with a racing exhaust and some stickier tyres.

CLASSIC BEAUTY

It is the CB400's styling, however, which has given it a timeless appeal. The spectacular chromed exhaust system has four meandering header pipes, which snake their way round the lacquered alloy engine, towards a large collector box and megaphone silencer. A slabby fuel tank, large chrome-rimmed headlight and chrome mudguards further enhance the classic café racer styling.

For all its attractive design and sparkling performance, the CB400 Four was an expensive machine to produce, and it was replaced in 1977 by cheaper but less impressive twin-cylinder designs, the CB400 Dream and Super Dream. But despite its comparatively short model life, the 400 Supersport has far outlived its successors in the hearts of motorcyclists and is a common sight at classic bike fairs and concours restoration parades.

Honda CB400 Four Supersport

Top speed:	167km/h (104mph)
Engine type:	408cc (25ci), a/c inline-four eight-valve, SOHC
Max power:	28kw (37bhp) @ 9000rpm
Frame type:	steel-tube cradle
Tyre sizes:	front 90/90 18, rear 110/90 18
Final drive:	chain
Gearbox:	six-speed
Weight:	178kg (392lb)

Honda CBR600F

Honda's longest-running sportsbike model, the CBR600F is perhaps the perfect sporting 600, as effective at world-class racing as it is at touring, commuting or pleasure-riding.

The CBR600F has a built-in immobilizer, which prevents the bike being started without the correct digitally chipped key. A code on the key chip must match the code in the fuel injection ECU.

A fully adjustable rear monoshock unit provides excellent damping on road or track. The remote reservoir can be seen just below the seat.

Like all CBR600 models, the FX uses an inline-four, water-cooled, 16-valve engine. It was the last model to use carburettors, later versions using fuel injection.

The aluminium swingarm is internally braced, with a cast pivot section. It is mounted to both the frame and the engine cases, which gives extra rigidity to the chassis.

An integrated one-piece dashboard comprises electronic digital and analogue displays for speed, engine revs, engine temperature and low fuel.

The two black intake tubes below the headlight direct cool, dense air into the sealed airbox, increasing peak power.

JAPAN

JAPAN

The 600cc (37ci) supersports class is, without doubt, the most important class of the modern sportsbike era. The combination of good performance and low cost makes a 600 sports bike the choice for thousands of riders, and the battle for market share ensures manufacturers strive to develop these machines.

The most successful of these 600 sports bikes is Honda's CBR600F. From its launch in 1987 as a fully faired, 60kw (80bhp) sportster (called the Hurricane in some markets), the CBR consistently topped both sales charts and press road tests as the best in class, combining all-round usability with genuine sporting potential.

This 1999 FX model was the first CBR600 with an aluminium twin-beam frame. Previous versions of the sporting 600 used heavier steel-tube perimeter frames.

But by 1998, the CBR was coming under pressure. The increasing leisure-biased nature of motorcycling meant practicality was becoming less important in the 600 class. Instead, machines such as Suzuki's GSX-R600 had moved towards the sportier end of the spectrum, with an exciting, cutting-edge race-ready chassis and engine. Honda's steel-framed, pillion-friendly CBR could still compete on the road, but was being left behind in track performance.

ALL-ROUND PERFORMANCE

So in 1999 came a new CBR, with an aluminium twin-beam frame and uprated engine. With its dry weight down to 170kg (375lb) and power up to a claimed 81kw (109bhp), the 1999 CBR600 FX model did improve performance. A stiffer, lighter frame offered more precise handling, adjustable race suspension allowed fine-tuning of the ride and new four-piston caliper brakes gave race-quality stopping power.

However, the Honda CBR600F maintained its reputation as an all-round machine: despite the sportier chassis, the new model retained a pillion grabrail, large dual seat and a comfortable riding position, as well as a centre stand.

Later models incorporated a fuel injection system, further improving performance and reducing emissions.

Honda CBR600F

Top speed:	266km/h (165mph)
Engine type:	599cc (37.ci), l/c inline-four, 16-valve, DOHC
Max power:	81kw (109bhp) @12,500rpm
Frame type:	aluminium twin spar
Tyre sizes:	front 120/70 17, rear 180/55 17
Final drive:	chain
Gearbox:	six-speed
Weight:	170kg (375lb)

Honda CB600F Hornet

The Hornet 600 combines the classy style and sporting performance of an urban café machine with the practicality and value of a middleweight roadster.

Chromed instrument pods hold the bare minimum, with just a speedometer, tachometer and indicator lights.

The Hornet engine derives from the CBR600F sportsbike engine. Smaller, 34mm (1.3in) carburettors and different intake and exhaust dimensions improve midrange power. Digital ignition gives precise spark timing.

The twin-piston sliding caliper brakes were initially criticized for poor performance. Later models had black calipers instead of the gold ones shown, and offered better performance.

The rear monoshock is a budget-specification model, adjustable for preload only.

The downpipes are stainless steel, and a high-level silencer runs below the pillion seat, echoing the style of the Japan-only Honda Hornet 250 model.

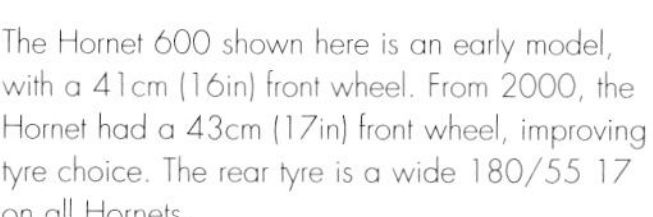

The Hornet 600 shown here is an early model, with a 41cm (16in) front wheel. From 2000, the Hornet had a 43cm (17in) front wheel, improving tyre choice. The rear tyre is a wide 180/55 17 on all Hornets.

Inspired by a 250cc (15ci) version available in Japan only, the Hornet 600 was Honda's entry into the vital middleweight budget roadster market of the late 1990s. Largely defined by Suzuki's GSF600 Bandit in 1995, this budget class was typified by an older generation 600cc (37ci) sportsbike engine fitted into a cheap yet effective chassis and sold at a price below cutting-edge 600cc (37ci) sports bikes.

To this end, the Hornet used the inline-four, 16-valve, water-cooled engine from

With the fuel tank and side panels removed, the simple square tube-steel frame can be seen running along from the steering head to the rear subframe section.

the firm's CBR600 sports bike. Smaller carburettors and other engine modifications increased the engine's midrange, but it was still a comparatively revvy engine, making the most of its power higher up in the rev range. This engine was mounted in a steel-tube backbone frame, allowing the engine to be seen in its entirety, without being hidden by side frame tubes or plastic panels.

CITY RIDING

The Hornet's suspension is capable, if rather basic, with conventional 41mm (1.6in) front forks and a cantilever-type rear monoshock. The twin-piston caliper front brakes were borrowed from the CBR600 and were also basic. Indeed, Honda fitted pads with slightly less bite, to make the brakes less sudden in operation for novice riders. Compared with those on Yamaha's Fazer, the Hornet's brakes had much less power and progression.

'Naked' bikes such as the CB600F Hornet are in their element in cities, where the little Honda excels. Its quick steering, light weight and compliant suspension make short work of traffic jams, bumpy cobbled streets and other hazards of the urban traffic landscape. The riding position seats the rider upright, all the better to spot hazards ahead and a bonus in city conditions, and the narrow frontal aspect means that the bike squeezes through small gaps with ease.

Honda CB600F Hornet

Top speed:	224km/h (140mph)
Engine type:	599cc (37ci), l/c inline-four, 16-valve, DOHC
Max power:	70kw (94bhp) @ 12,000rpm
Frame type:	steel-tube backbone
Tyre sizes:	front 120/70 17, rear 180/55 17
Final drive:	chain
Gearbox:	six-speed
Weight:	176kg (387lb)

JAPAN

Honda CB600F S Hornet

Intended to offer a more practical option, Honda's CB600F S Hornet has all the attitude of its naked sibling, with a neat half-fairing.

From the 2000 model year (when the S was introduced), Honda fitted the Hornet 600 with a 43cm (17in) front wheel. The rear wheel, however, remained the same 43cm (17in) part, with a 180/55 tyre.

Although the CB600F S is a more comfortable tourer, with its protective fairing, the fuel range is still insufficient. The steel tank holds only 16l (3.5gal), limiting range to about 225km (140 miles).

In 2000, both the faired and unfaired Hornets received uprated brakes, with new pads and different hoses, to improve stopping power.

The Hornet's exhaust system precludes fitting a main centre stand, so there is only a side stand. This makes maintenance and roadside wheel changes more difficult.

Rearview mirrors are new fairing-mounted types, rather than the chrome stalk handlebar-mounted mirrors of the unfaired bike.

This clear lens headlight design uses an all-plastic construction for light weight. It is similar to the firm's Firestorm and Transalp headlight designs.

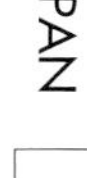

Honda's unfaired Hornet 600 had been on sale for two years when the Japanese firm unveiled this half-faired variant of the budget middleweight roadster. The basic Hornet had been a successful model for Honda, thanks to an attractive design and strong performance. However, it lost out to more practical, faired machines such as Yamaha's Fazer 600: riders who needed to travel long distances at speed, or in all weathers, preferred the convenience of a small fairing

The cockpit features racy instruments with a carbon-fibre effect finish. These are based on the electronic parts from Honda's VTR1000 Firestorm.

and windscreen. Additionally, the unfaired Hornet was not really suitable for touring work or other two-up duties, although the strong engine and comfortable riding position stood in its favour.

The decision to fit a 'bikini'-type mini fairing seemed obvious, and so few observers were surprised to see the new model on show at the 1999 Milan show. The new body panels included a clear-lens type headlight, which looked similar to that fitted to other bikes in Honda's line-up.

EXTRA STABILITY

The fairing was not the only modification made to the Hornet. The faired bike came with a 43cm (17in) front wheel (as did the unfaired bike for 2000), rather than the 41cm (16in) part of the previous model. This improved tyre choice, as well as adding stability to the steering. The new Hornet 'S' also had a new dashboard fitted to the frame-mounted fairing.

The new fairing truly added a new dimension to the Hornet's abilities, although it was not such a large success as the unfaired bike. Some Hornet fans thought the extra bodywork detracted from the naked bike's styling, and the faired bike was still less practical than its competitors, particularly Yamaha's Fazer, which had a more flexible engine and much better fuel range.

Honda CB600F S Hornet

Top speed:	232km/h (145mph)
Engine type:	599cc (37ci), l/c inline-four, 16-valve, DOHC
Max power:	70kw (94bhp) @ 12,000rpm
Frame type:	steel-tube backbone
Tyre sizes:	front 120/70 17, rear 180/55 17
Final drive:	chain
Gearbox:	six-speed
Weight:	178kg (392lb)

JAPAN

HONDA NR750

Probably the most complex, ahead-of-its-time motorcycle ever made, Honda's exotic NR750 is a beautifully exquisite piece of corporate chest-puffing.

The gorgeous tinted windscreen is coated with a layer of iridescent titanium.

The ignition key is made from nickel silver and carbon fibre.

The exquisitely shaped fairing, fuel tank and seat unit are all made from hand-laid carbon fibre.

The PGM-FI engine management system uses a 16-bit CPU and has eight injectors, one for both of the intake ports in each oval cylinder.

A special articulated cover pivots out with the hidden side stand, and the red paint was specially developed for the NR.

The NR750's dashboard included a 'head-up' display, which projected an LCD display up onto the screen in front of the rider.

The aerodynamically shaped mirrors incorporate the turn signals. The same mirrors were later used on Honda's CBR1100XX Super Blackbird.

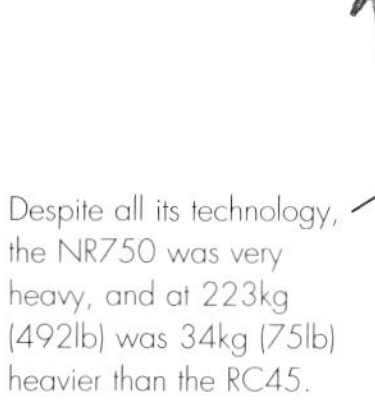

Despite all its technology, the NR750 was very heavy, and at 223kg (492lb) was 34kg (75lb) heavier than the RC45.

The NR750 cost around £37,500 when launched. Only around 200 were made, and the bike was on sale for exactly one year.

A glance at the NR750 gives little clue to the age of the design: the NR first appeared in 1990 as a marshal bike at the Suzuka Eight Hour race. It went on sale in 1992, being produced in limited numbers for one year only - around 200 were made.

The NR750 was developed from Honda's attempts to continue racing four-stroke engines in Grand Prix racing. The NR500 used an oval-piston design to compete with the two-stroke designs which had taken over Grand Prix racing, but it suffered

An amazingly complicated eight-into-four-into-two-into-one-into-two exhaust system is made from stainless steel and is normally totally hidden by the bodywork, apart from the underseat exits.

many development problems and was not successful. Honda finally gave in and produced two-stroke GP racers, but the groundwork done by the NR500 team resulted in arguably the most advanced road bike ever produced.

PEAK PERFORMANCE

The most impressive part of the NR750 is the engine. Its oval-piston V-four layout uses two conrods, four inlet valves, four exhaust valves, two spark plugs, two fuel injectors and one 'spam tin' shaped oval piston per 'cylinder' - impressive in 2003, astounding in 1992. Producing peak power of 93kw (125bhp) at 14,000rpm, the NR's engine was supremely unstressed - tuned versions were reputed to make over 112kw (150bhp), amazing power for a 750cc (46ci) engine.

The chassis was rather unremarkable next to the engine, although its single-sided swingarm and upside-down forks were unusual in the early 1990s. The swooping bodywork is unforgettable, though. And while the NR750 was a cul-de-sac for Honda in that no more oval-piston engines have been made, it nevertheless set design trends for the rest of the decade. Underseat exhausts, indicators in mirrors, single-sided swingarms and louvred fairings have all become common sights on sports bikes in the years since 1992.

Honda NR750

Top speed:	257km/h (160mph)
Engine type:	748cc (46ci), l/c 90° V-four, 32-valve, DOHC, oval piston
Max power:	93kw (125bhp) @14,000rpm
Frame type:	aluminium twin spar
Tyre sizes:	front 130/70 16, rear 180/55 17
Final drive:	chain
Gearbox:	six-speed
Weight:	223kg (492lb)

Honda RVF750R RC45

Honda was determined to win the World Superbike championship with a V-four, despite the rules favouring twin-cylinder bikes. The RC45 managed it, but only once.

The RC45 was the first Honda road bike to use upside-down front forks, fully adjustable Showa parts. The Japanese firm avoids using USD forks, except on its highest-specification race-replica machines.

The PGM-FI fuel injection system had an adjustment box with four small screws, which controlled mixture strength at various throttle openings. Serious tuners need factory-only race kit parts to get the most from the engine.

The RC45 has a close ratio gearbox, with a very tall first gear. Maximum speed in first gear is around 135km/h (85mph), and the rider has to slip the clutch carefully to pull away.

The cam gear train which operated the quad camshafts was moved to the end of the crankshaft, allowing a narrower engine with less internal friction.

As with the CBR900RR, Honda fitted the RC45 with a 41cm (16in) front wheel. The Honda race kit, however, used a 43cm (17in) wheel to improve tyre choice.

From an engineering perspective, the V-four engine layout may be the ideal motorcycle engine format. Compact and powerful, with a centralized mass, a V-four was the choice of two-stroke 500GP bikes throughout the 1980s and 1990s.

On the road, however, it is only really Honda which has used the format widely. From unfavourable beginnings in its VF range, the Honda V-four engine grew into a powerful, reliable and soulful engine in the late 1980s. A 750 version powered the

The RC45 motor was all-new when launched and shared none of its architecture with the older RC30 design. The stroke was much shorter at 46mm (1.8in) for higher revs, increasing ultimate maximum power.

legendary VFR750R RC30 to countless race victories between 1987 and 1993, but 1994 saw Honda launch a new V-four race replica, the RVF750R RC45. Like the RC30, the RC45 was sold as a homologation bike - in other words, it was sold in limited numbers to allow its use in production-based racing. Race series such as World Superbike require competing machines to be based on road bikes available to the public.

COMPETITIVE TECHNOLOGY

Also like the RC30, the RC45 used a V-four 749cc (46ci) engine in an aluminium twin-beam frame and single-sided swingarm. But both engine and chassis were heavily overhauled: the engine had electronic fuel injection, a shorter stroke and a narrower layout. The chassis wore upside-down forks, which Honda reserved for pure competition machines.

The RC45 was hugely expensive: it cost almost £18,000 ($26,000) when launched in the UK in 1994, more than twice as expensive as a CBR900RR FireBlade at the time. But its sublime chassis and strong, torquey engine made for a supreme riding experience. Despite its advanced technology, the RC45 failed to repeat the success of the RC30, although it did win the World Superbike championship once in 1997, ridden by American racer John Kocinski.

Honda RVF750R RC45

Top speed:	257km/h (160mph)
Engine type:	749cc (46ci), l/c 90° V-four, 16-valve, DOHC
Max power:	88kw (118bhp) @ 12,000rpm
Frame type:	aluminium twin spar
Tyre sizes:	front 130/70 16, rear 190/50 17
Final drive:	chain
Gearbox:	six-speed
Weight:	189kg (417lb)

Honda XRV750 Africa Twin

With the styling of a competition desert racer, Honda's Africa Twin is an imposing off-roader. For most riders, however, it is best kept on the Tarmac.

The Africa Twin has a small trip computer mounted above the speedometer and tachometer, which is designed to look like the complex navigation systems of real desert racers.

Both the front forks and the rear monoshock have extra long travel, to absorb large bumps and dips in the terrain.

A large aluminium engine bashplate is designed to protect the bottom of the engine from impacts with the ground and sharp rocks.

A 53cm (21in) front wheel and 43cm (17in) rear hold tyres styled to be off-road, with many tread cuts and grippy knobs of rubber, but more suited to use on metalled roads or firm trails.

A pair of plastic handguards is designed to protect the rider's fingers and the bike's levers from impact by branches. The guards also offer extra weather protection for the hands.

Corrugated flexible rubber tubes protect the sliding tubes of the front forks from dirt and stones.

While bikes such as Honda's XRV750 Africa Twin have all the appearance and styling of open-class off-road racers, they have, in reality, little off-road capability. Like the large four- wheel drive, off-road styled cars beloved of well-heeled city dwellers, these big trailies are almost universally restricted to use on Tarmac. Excessive weight, road-pattern tyres and extensive, easily damaged bodywork all make the Africa Twin totally unsuited to serious off-road riding.

The 52° V-twin engine is developed from the same basic unit as Honda's Transalp 600 and the NT650 Revere. It has three valves for each cylinder, two inlet and one exhaust.

That said, its design features are useful. Indeed, soft, long travel suspension, a high riding position and tractable engine are all desirable attributes for bikes used primarily in urban areas or as gentle tourers - which is where Honda's Africa Twin excels. While its name hints at aggressive, desert-racing ability, the XRV is in fact much more at home on city streets or continental motorways. Its softly tuned, 742cc (45ci), 52 degree V-twin engine produces a friendly 44kw (59bhp), the extensive bodywork keeps the windblast off the rider and a large 23l (5gal) fuel tank gives an easy 400km (250 miles) between fill-ups. There is ample space on the comfortable dual seat for a pillion to journey in comfort, and a rear rack helps with carrying luggage.

LONG-RUNNING SUCCESS

Less impressive are the dual front disc brakes, which offer rather mediocre performance, although the soft forks and trail tyres would hinder the efforts of more powerful brakes. The extremely high seat height is also off-putting for shorter riders.

While never a massive sales success for Honda, the Africa Twin is one of the firm's longest-running models, remaining mostly unchanged since its launch in 1989. It was also in limited production as a 650cc (40ci) version in some markets in 1988.

Honda XRV750 Africa Twin

Top speed:	177km/h (110mph)
Engine type:	742cc (45ci), l/c 52° V-twin, six-valve, SOHC
Max power:	44kw (59bhp) @ 7500rpm
Frame type:	steel-tube single cradle
Tyre sizes:	front 90/90 21, rear 140/80 17
Final drive:	chain
Gearbox:	five-speed
Weight:	205kg (452lb)

Honda VFR800

With almost two decades of refinement behind it, Honda's VFR is an intensely developed sports tourer, with enough performance and comfort for any rider.

Honda's Dual CBS linked brakes combine the front and rear braking systems, to give improved performance for less experienced riders.

The VFR800 was the first mainstream Honda to use fuel injection. Its PGM-FI system was based on that used on the RC45 and NR750.

A compact, powerful V-four engine is based on the WSB-winning RC45 racer. Its quad camshafts are driven by gears, operating four valves per cylinder.

The VFR800 uses Honda's 'pivotless' frame design; the rear swingarm is mounted directly to the engine cases.

A further model update in 2002 featured a variable valve VTEC engine and optional ABS brakes.

The bolt-on grabrails can be removed quickly and the pillion seat replaced by a sporty seat cover, for solo riding.

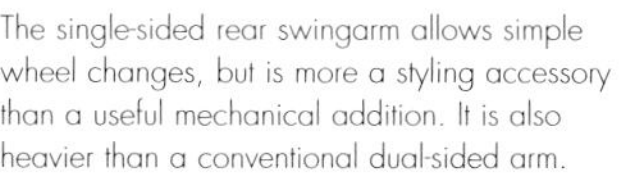
The single-sided rear swingarm allows simple wheel changes, but is more a styling accessory than a useful mechanical addition. It is also heavier than a conventional dual-sided arm.

In the mid-1990s, Honda had a virtual stranglehold on the main motorcycle classes. Its CBR900RR FireBlade was the best litre-class sports bike, the CBR600F was at the top of the 600 class and the VFR750 ruled the sports-touring roost.

But in 1997, Honda took the opportunity to lift the VFR even higher above the competition. The Japanese engineers designed an all-new 782cc (48ci) engine, based on the World Superbike-winning RC45 engine, and fitted it in a revamped

The VFR's side-mounted radiators seen here allow the engine to be mounted further forward in the chassis, improving handling. Air is ducted through the fairing and sucked out through the side, further improving aerodynamic performance.

sporting chassis. The result was impressive: the new fuel-injected engine offered even more refined power and torque than the old 750, while the new chassis maintained the comfort and practicality of the old bike, yet still added a healthy dose of extra performance. Honda fitted its new Dual-CBS linked brakes, which gave better brake balance for inexperienced riders, while the advanced PGM-FI fuel injection system gave smooth, fuss-free power delivery throughout the rev range.

OUTCLASSING THE COMPETITION

The VFR800 had the ability to easily travel 800km (500 miles) two-up in a day, with luggage, then spend the following day scratching hard on a twisty Alpine back road, keeping up with more focused sporting machinery. These tough attributes are the hallmark of a true sports-touring machine.

Competition for the older bike had come from machines such as Ducati's ST2 and BMW's R1100S, both of which were outclassed by the VFR750's performance. But it proved well for Honda that it did overhaul the VFR - the following year saw strong new competition from Triumph's Sprint ST and BMW's R1100S. Both these new models ran the new 800 close in terms of practicality, and the Triumph was able to match the VFR800 in terms of performance, too.

Honda VFR800

Top speed:	256km/h (160mph)
Engine type:	782cc (48ci), l/c 90° V-four, 16-valve, DOHC
Max power:	80kw (107bhp) @ 10,500rpm
Frame type:	aluminium twin spar
Tyre sizes:	front 120/70 17, rear 180/55 17
Final drive:	chain
Gearbox:	six-speed
Weight:	218kg (480lb)

Honda CBR900RR FireBlade

Honda's CBR900RR FireBlade is the definitive sports bike of the 1990s. Its blend of extreme power and fine rider control took superbike performance to a new level.

The front forks resemble upside-down parts, but are conventional items, albeit with wide, stiff 45mm (1.7in) stanchions.

The stubby, wide steel fuel tank holds 18l (3.96 gal) of unleaded petrol.

Four-piston Nissin calipers and dual 310mm (12.2 in) floating discs provide excellent stopping power.

The twin-spar aluminium frame is unremarkable, apart from its light weight and high stiffness.

This 1998 FireBlade has a minimalist racing type dashboard, with a speedometer, tachometer and warning lights mounted in a lightweight panel.

Small, round holes in the FireBlade top fairing are claimed to improve aerodynamic performance and manoeuvrability.

The front wheel was a 41cm (16in) part until 2000, when it was replaced by a more conventional 43cm (17in) wheel. The rear wheel is a 43cm (17in) part, with a 180/55 tyre, which grew to a 190/50 in 2000.

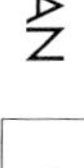

If there is one motorcycle which can be said to define the modern superbike, it is Honda's CBR900RR FireBlade. Launched in 1992 to almost hysterical acclaim from the press, it quickly became clear that Honda had built a machine far beyond the abilities of its peers. It was to be five years before any other manufacturer came near to the performance of the FireBlade.

At the heart of the CBR900's success was an integrated approach to its design, together with a commitment to reduce

The 1998 FireBlade engine was a 919cc (56ci) capacity inline-four, 16-valve design, with 38mm (1.5in) CV carburettors. From 2000, capacity increased to 929cc (57ci), then 954cc (58ci) in 2002. Fuel injection replaced the carburettors in 2000.

weight as well as increase power over its predecessors. The result was a tiny bike, weighing just 185kg (408lb) and producing 91kw (122bhp): its nearest competitor, Yamaha's FZR1000 EXUP, produced 93kw (125bhp), but was more than 35kg (77lb) heavier at 209kg (461lb). Even Honda's own 600cc (37ci) sports bike, the CBR600, was no lighter than the new FireBlade.

REDUCING WEIGHT

The Honda's lightweight design improved handling, braking and acceleration, and began a trend towards lighter sports bikes. There was no radical technology involved in the process - the frame was a standard twin-beam aluminium design, and the engine was a 16-valve, DOHC water-cooled design. What was different was Honda's success in shrinking and lightening the design of both the engine and the chassis. However it was achieved, the CBR900RR is one of the classic sports bikes: fast, dynamic, exhilarating.

Updates every couple of years gradually improved the FireBlade. Its engine capacity increased from 893cc (54ci) to 918cc (56ci) in 1996, then 929cc (56ci) in 2000 and 954cc (58ci) in 2002. Weight also dropped from the original 185kg (408lb) to 168kg (370lb) in 2002. Despite these updates, the FireBlade lost its top spot first to Yamaha's R1 in 1997, then Suzuki's GSX-R1000 in 2001.

Honda CBR900RR Fireblade

Top speed:	272km/h (170mph)
Engine type:	918cc (56ci), l/c inline-four, 16 valve, DOHC
Max power:	95kw (128bhp) @11250rpm
Frame type:	aluminium twin spar
Tyre sizes:	front 130/70 16, rear 190/50 17
Final drive:	chain
Gearbox:	six-speed
Weight:	180kg (396lb)

Honda CBR1000F

The predecessor to the Super Blackbird, Honda's CBR1000F was a plush, luxurious sports tourer with a smooth, powerful engine, massive top speed and a capable chassis.

A large reserve-fuel tap mounted at the front of the dual seat is easy to use with gloves.

The CBR1000's all-enveloping bodywork gives excellent aerodynamic performance and hides the rather messy frame and engine underneath. The vents below the windscreen smooth the airflow over the rider.

The CBS linked brakes were not appreciated by all owners, some of whom bypassed the system with aftermarket parts, returning their bikes to a conventional brake setup.

The black-finished four-into-two exhaust system gives a broad spread of power and a pleasant edge to the smooth engine note.

Clear, simple analogue dials display speed, engine rpm and temperature.

The fairing-mounted mirrors give an excellent view of the road behind.

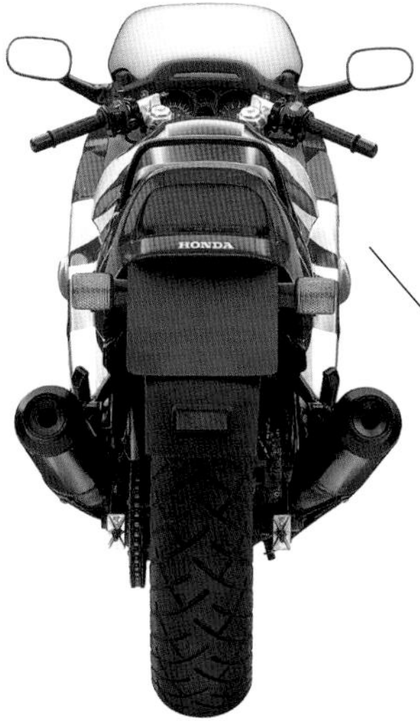

The dual-bulb, single-lens headlight gives amazingly bright illumination at night.

The dual seat is extremely broad, spacious and comfortable for both rider and pillion. A large grabrail gives a secure handhold for the passenger.

Although it was launched by Honda at the same time as the extremely successful CBR600, the CBR1000 never enjoyed the same long life or showroom success. When it was first presented to the public in 1987, its fully faired bodywork, powerful 998cc (61ci) engine and sports chassis placed it at the head of Honda's sportsbike range. Compared with the opposition of the day – Kawasaki's GPz1000RX, Suzuki's GSX-R1100 and Yamaha's FJ1200 – the CBR was an

With the bodywork removed, the steel-tube perimeter frame looks rather insubstantial. But it offers perfectly acceptable stiffness, at the expense of excess weight.

advanced design with better performance. Its inline-four 16-valve engine was incredibly smooth, and its full fairing made it look suitably futuristic and modern. While the first FH model's suspension and brakes are rather archaic by modern standards, the conventional forks, rear monoshock and dual twin-piston front brake calipers were at the top of the class in 1987.

As the CBR evolved through the late 1980s and 1990s, it gradually turned into a polished sports tourer. The fairing was reshaped into a more modern design, while retaining its great wind protection for rider and pillion. The engine received detail updates, but remained essentially the same unit.

COMBINED BRAKING

One area which did receive Honda's attention was the brakes. In 1993, the CBR1000F debuted Honda's Dual CBS combined braking system. This setup used a series of hoses and control valves to link both the front and rear brake circuits together. So when the rider pulled the front brake lever, the back brake also operated. Similarly, pressing the rear brake lever operated part of the front brake system as well as the rear. Dual CBS was designed to improve stopping abilities, particularly for less experienced riders, but it did not meet universal acclaim among owners.

Honda CBR1000F

Top speed:	266km/h (165mph)
Engine type:	998cc (61ci), l/c inline-four, 16-valve, DOHC
Max power:	101kw (135bhp) @ 9500rpm
Frame type:	steel-tube perimeter
Tyre sizes:	front 120/70 17, rear 170/60 17
Final drive:	chain
Gearbox:	six-speed
Weight:	235kg (518lb)

Honda CBX1000

A relic from the extrovert years of the 1970s, Honda's CBX1000 is an audacious superbike, dominated by its six-cylinder, 24-valve, 1000cc (61ci) engine.

The CBX engine is primarily air-cooled by the fins on the engine. But a small oil radiator below the headstock helps keep the engine temperature down during harder riding.

Honda fitted the CBX with a capacious 20l (4.4gal) fuel tank, giving a range of more than 270km (168 miles).

Small, solid discs, and single-piston brake calipers all round, give the CBX1000 poor stopping power by modern standards.

The engine was extremely wide, so Honda moved the alternator behind the cylinders, below the carburettors, to make it narrower.

While not standard fitment, most owners fitted steel crash bars to their machines, to protect the vulnerable engine in minor spills.

The telescopic front forks and twin rear shocks are rather weak and underdamped. The later touring version of the CBX used a monoshock rear suspension system, improving handling significantly.

The CBX was fitted with fabricated Comstar-type wheels, with rather narrow tyres.

One of the technological dead-ends down which various Japanese motorcycle firms went in the late 1970s was the six-cylinder motorcycle. Both Honda and Kawasaki produced in-line sixes: Kawasaki's water-cooled Z1300 was released in 1979, a year after Honda's air-cooled six-cylinder CBX1000.

Both bikes were launched as sports bikes, although both the Honda and the Kawasaki were rather large and heavy for a sporting role. The CBX had a more modern, four valves per cylinder design, although the engine remained air-cooled, unlike the liquid-cooled Kawasaki. Designed by one of Honda's race engineers, Soichiro Irimajiri,

Under the large fuel tank, a steel-tube spine frame curves over the engine from the steering head down to the swingarm pivot. This shows off the bike's stunning engine to best effect.

the CBX engine was a technical marvel, with race-type lightweight valve gear and high-performance internals, aping Honda's legendary six-cylinder 250cc (15ci) GP bikes of the 1960s.

An inline-six engine boasts perfect natural balance, so the CBX's smoothness was to be expected. However, its 78kw (105bhp) peak power output was among the highest available, and the strong power delivery allowed relaxed, fast progress to a top speed of almost 208km/h (130mph).

A RELAUNCH

The size and width of the CBX engine encouraged Honda to use a then-unusual spine-frame layout, which used the engine as a stressed member. The conventional suspension and triple-disc brake systems were typical high-end parts of the time

The CBX handled very well, but it was still heavy and expensive compared with less exotic four-cylinder sports bikes such as Suzuki's GS1000 and Kawasaki's Z1000. To that end, Honda relaunched the CBX1000 in 1981 as a grand touring machine, with a large fairing, hard luggage and a new monoshock rear suspension system. The new bike had better handling, but less performance, and Honda's four-cylinder CB900 range took over the flagship sportsbike role, the CBX1000 finally ceasing production in 1982.

Honda CBX1000

Top speed:	208km/h (130mph)
Engine type:	1047cc (64ci), a/c inline-six, 24-valve, DOHC
Max power:	78kw (105bhp) @ 9000rpm
Frame type:	steel-tube spine
Tyre sizes:	front 100/90 19, rear 120/90 18
Final drive:	chain
Gearbox:	five-speed
Weight:	247kg (545lb)

JAPAN

Honda VTR1000 Firestorm

A powerful, compact V-twin sports bike for the road, Honda's stylish Firestorm was a head-on assault on Ducati's sporting V-twin superbikes, with better performance and advanced design.

The Firestorm's half fairing is less protective than fully faired machines, but still gives good aerodynamic performance.

The Firestorm's fuel tank was very small when it was launched, holding just 16l (3.5 gal). In 2001 came a larger 19l (4.2 gal) tank, but range was still poor at around 200km (125 miles).

Side-mounted radiators improve cooling and simplify the engine mounting and front exhaust routing.

A small, grey plastic cowling smooths the engine's lines and hides the oil filter from sight.

The small, triangular mirrors are aerodynamic and stylish, but do not provide a great view of the road behind.

A large capacity air cleaner box sits above the engine, providing a large reservoir of air to ensure steady power delivery.

A model update in 2001 meant a bigger fuel tank, new instruments, revised fork settings, higher handlebars and an immobilizer.

Until the late 1990s, most Japanese sports bikes used four-cylinder engines. Honda used both inline and V-four engines in bikes such as the RC45, CBR600 and CBR900RR FireBlade. But the success of Ducati's V-twin 916 superbike, notably in World Superbike competition, encouraged Japanese firms to investigate their own V-twin-powered sports bikes.

Honda's VTR1000 Firestorm (known as the Super Hawk in the USA) was the first to arrive on the market, at the beginning of 1997. It was an advanced design, with an aluminium truss twin-beam frame, adjustable

While the VTR's aluminium frame is stiff enough for road use, its 'pivotless' design, which uses the engine cases as the swingarm pivot, is not stiff enough for racing use. Some tuners added aluminium braces between the frame and pivot to improve track handling.

sports suspension and a high-tech, water-cooled, eight-valve, 90° V-twin engine. It was both lighter and more powerful than Ducati's 916, as well as costing 50 per cent less than the Italian bike, making it an instant success in showrooms.

EFFECTIVE DESIGN

The Firestorm was a success on the road, too. Producing 82kw (110bhp), its engine delivers flexible, torquey power delivery, with a strong punch pulling out of corners. Large 48mm (1.9in) carburettors and the twin-silencer exhaust system optimize midrange power, while allowing a respectable top-end urge, although the Firestorm engine has a softer power delivery than some of its rivals.

The chassis is effective, if unsophisticated: both the forks and rear shock are budget road parts, rather than exotic adjustable racing versions. Similarly, the dual four-piston front brake calipers are workmanlike designs, doing a good job with no fuss or show. A stylish, sculpted half-fairing protects the rider from windblast and incorporates the side-mounted radiators. These are designed to position the engine closer to the front wheel, allowing a shorter chassis. A stepped dual seat provides rather minimal pillion accommodation: the Firestorm is best kept as a solo sports touring machine.

Honda VTR1000 Firestorm

Top speed:	272km/h (170mph)
Engine type:	996cc (61ci), l/c 90° V-twin, eight-valve, DOHC
Max power:	82kw (110bhp) @ 9000rpm
Frame type:	aluminium trellis twin spar
Tyre sizes:	front 120/70 17, rear 180/55 17
Final drive:	chain
Gearbox:	six-speed
Weight:	192kg (422lb)

Honda VTR1000 SP-1

Built as a base bike to win World Superbike races with, Honda's SP-1 is an exotic, V-twin race-replica, with cutting-edge chassis and engine technologies.

The SP-1 proved to be a potent package, on the road and on track. Texan racer Colin Edwards won the 2000 WSB championship in the SP-1's inaugural year.

The SP-1's four camshafts are driven by gears from the crankshaft, rather than a chain, for improved valve timing control at high engine speeds.

The front Nissin four-piston calipers are mounted to the forks by aluminium mount plates. This is to allow their replacement by racing brakes without requiring complex fitting work.

The SP-1 uses twin 54mm (2.25in) throttle bodies, with two injectors per cylinder. Each injector has a four-jet nozzle for improved fuel atomization.

This air intake actually passes through the frame's steering head, in order to allow the most direct path for cool, high-pressure air to pass from the front of the fairing into the sealed airbox.

The stainless-steel two-into-two exhaust system has steeply upswept silencers to improve ground clearance.

Honda released an SP-2 model in 2002 with WSB-inspired updates, including lighter wheels.

Honda launched its VTR1000 SP-1 in 1999 with one aim: to win the World Superbike championship. Ducati's 916-based range was sweeping the board, and Honda's four-cylinder RC45 could not compete with the lighter 1000cc (61ci) V-twin class, despite winning the World Superbike championship in 1997. The VTR1000 Firestorm, launched two years before, was unsuitable for racing, so a new machine was needed to provide the base for a successful competition machine.

A massive fabricated aluminium swingarm uses 'Yagura'-type bracing for extra stiffness without excessive weight.

Dubbed the VTR1000 SP-1, the new Honda WSB contender used an eight-valve, DOHC, 90° V-twin engine, similar in layout to the Firestorm, but with 90 per cent of the engine internals replaced by uprated parts. The bore was increased and stroke decreased, to allow a higher rpm limit; new ceramic-plated bores reduce both weight and friction; and the engine covers are made from lightweight magnesium.

RACING POWER

The Firestorm's chassis was not designed for race use, so the SP-1's chassis is totally new. The most striking aspect of the twin-beam aluminium framed chassis is the large air intake between the headlights. This novel intake apart, the chassis is conventional: fully adjustable Showa upside-down forks and monoshock, heavily braced swingarm and dual four-piston front brake calipers.

Riding the VTR1000 SP-1 can be a very satisfying experience, depending on the circumstances. On a race track, or a flowing, twisty road, it is superb. The engine has a powerful punch from low down in the rev range, the brakes are excellent and the suspension is superbly damped. If the SP-1 is taken into town or used for distance riding, however, it is less impressive. The fuel consumption is high, and the engine has a rather jerky power delivery at low rpm.

Honda VTR1000 SP-1

Top speed:	274km/h (170mph)
Engine type:	999cc (61ci), l/c 90° V-twin, eight-valve, DOHC
Max power:	101kw (136bhp) @ 10,000rpm
Frame type:	aluminium twin spar
Tyre sizes:	front 120/70 17, rear 190/50 17
Final drive:	chain
Gearbox:	six-speed
Weight:	200kg (440lb)

JAPAN

Honda XL1000V Varadero

Honda's Varadero combines a VTR1000-based engine with an enduro-styled touring bike chassis to produce an effective mile-muncher with distinctive styling and sound performance.

A resin rack incorporates dual pillion grab handles and can be used as a mounting plate for an optional luggage topbox.

The Varadero's bodywork has unconventional styling, with a tall, sculpted fairing.

The Varadero has a pair of side-mounted engine radiators. These have been moved from the traditional location in front of the engine to provide more room for the exhaust system and allow the engine to be located further forward in the frame.

Offroad-style brushguards give extra weather protection for the rider's hands.

The extremely large fuel tank extends down either side of the bike, holding a capacious 25l (5.5 gal).

The Varadero uses Honda's Dual CBS brakes, which link the two front and one rear three-piston calipers together. When the rider pulls the front brake lever, two pistons of each front caliper and one on the rear are operated. When the rear brake is operated, two pistons operate on the rear caliper and one on each front caliper.

The Varadero is Honda's entry into the large-capacity touring trailbike market. Like BMW's R1150GS, it uses trailbike styling, but in a much more road-oriented package. Indeed, the styling and the long-travel suspension are the only real concessions to off-road use: the tyres, mudguards and ground clearance are up to only very gentle, green-lane use.

This is because the Varadero is really a touring machine. Powered by a retuned version of the VTR1000 Firestorm engine, it offers a long-distance package with 'adventure' styling and respectable

A stainless-steel exhaust system has large-capacity high-level twin silencers. These help improve power delivery while continuing the off-road styling theme.

performance. The engine has been fitted with smaller 42mm (1.6in) carburettors, pushing the power curve lower down the rev range, and a five-speed gearbox to suit the broader spread of power.

The Varadero chassis is largely unremarkable - a steel-tube cantilever-type frame links an aluminium rear swingarm to conventional 43mm (1.7in) front forks. The frame's 'pivotless' design uses the engine's crankcases to carry the swingarm pivot. Three-spoke aluminium wheels are fitted with very lightly trail-styled tubeless tyres, and the brakes are a variation on Honda's CBS linked braking system.

FUEL ECONOMY

The fuel tank is large and holds 25l (5.5 gal) of petrol. This does not, however, translate into a large fuel range - in fact, the Varadero shares the Firestorm's notorious thirsty nature and can average less than 10km/l (30mpg) on freeways.

For 2003, the Varadero (named after a Cuban seaside resort, strangely) received a comprehensive overhaul. To improve fuel economy, the engine was fitted with a PGM-FI fuel injection system, and the sixth gear was re-fitted. The bodywork was replaced by parts with more swooping curves, and a revised dashboard featured extra displays, including a fuel consumption gauge.

Honda XL1000V Varadero

Top speed:	216km/h (135mph)
Engine type:	996cc (61ci), l/c 90° V-twin, eight-valve, DOHC
Max power:	71kw (95bhp) @ 8000rpm
Frame type:	'pivotless' steel-tube cantilever
Tyre sizes:	front 110/80 19, rear 150/70 17
Final drive:	chain
Gearbox:	five-speed
Weight:	220kg (484lb)

JAPAN

HONDA CBR1100XX SUPER BLACKBIRD

With an extremely powerful 1100cc (67ci) engine and advanced aerodynamics, Honda's 280km/h (175mph) Super Blackbird was the world's fastest production bike when launched in 1996.

The Blackbird's ignition key contains a uniquely coded chip, matched to the fuel injection ECU, which is read by a radio antenna in the ignition switch. Without the correct key, the bike cannot be started.

The steel fuel tank holds an impressive 24l (5.3gal) of fuel, allowing more than 300km (187 miles) between fill-ups.

The Blackbird's brakes use Honda's unique Dual CBS system to link the front and rear brake circuits.

The engine incorporates dual balancer shafts to minimize vibrations and allows the engine to be solidly mounted in the frame, to increase chassis stiffness.

Borrowed from the NR750, the Blackbird's mirrors have the turn signals built in, reducing frontal area.

On early Blackbirds, the wind pressure at maximum speeds slightly pushed the front brake lever back, operating the brake light. Later versions had a slimmer, more streamlined lever.

A stainless-steel four-into-two exhaust system has cylinder link pipes to boost midrange drive.

JAPAN

Honda launched the CBR1100XX in 1996 to prepare for the phasing out of its ageing CBR1000F. Intended as an extremely fast sports tourer, the CBR1100XX was intended to take on Kawasaki's ZZ-R1100, which had dominated the unlimited-class sporting market since its launch in 1990. Based on CBR900RR design principles, the Super Blackbird is a very accomplished, civilized machine, despite its imposing top speed and the power output of its engine.

The first model introduced featured a carburetted engine, and the air intakes

In this stripped-down view, the Blackbird's pressurized air intake tubes can clearly be seen leading from the front fairing vents to the large-capacity airbox located above the engine.

below the headlight led to an oil cooler. But an updated model, released in 1999, switched to Honda's PGM-FI fuel injection and used these air inlets to feed a sealed ram-air intake system. These changes corrected a flat spot present in the first model's power delivery, as well as boosting top speed.

COMPACT AND DYNAMIC

The Blackbird's engine is a straightforward 16-valve inline-four DOHC design, most notable for its compactness and impressive power output - the fuel-injected machine produces almost 123kw (165bhp). Similarly, the chassis is typical of a Japanese sports bike, with an aluminium beam frame and sporty roadbike suspension parts.

But it is the detail design which makes the Blackbird work so well at speed. The sleek fairing is very aerodynamic, cocooning rider and passenger in a pocket of still air, while the distinctive 'stacked' headlight minimizes frontal area for less drag.

Riding the Super Blackbird is invigorating - power output is incredible; delivery is smooth and fuss-free. Very fast progress on motorways is easy, the engine making such riding a relaxed proposition. However, the Blackbird is also good for sporty riding, its power overcoming the shortcomings of the chassis as compared to a 'proper' sports bike.

Honda CBR1100XX Super Blackbird

Top speed:	288km/h (180mph)
Engine type:	1137cc (69ci), l/c inline-four, 16-valve, DOHC
Max power:	123kw (165bhp) @ 9500rpm
Frame type:	aluminium twin spar
Tyre sizes:	front 120/70 17, rear 180/55 17
Final drive:	chain
Gearbox:	six-speed
Weight:	224kg (493lb)

Honda ST1100A Pan European

Honda's heavyweight tourer was designed with the performance to cross countries in a day, while keeping the rider and pillion perfectly protected from the elements.

The 28l (6.15 gal) fuel tank is positioned behind the airbox and runs down below the riders seat, helping keep the centre of gravity low down.

The side-mounted panniers easily unclip to carry luggage into hotel rooms. An optional topbox mounts to the rear grabrail.

The ST1100 is incredibly well made and lasts many thousands of miles. Many fleet users choose it for this reason.

The ABS version of the Pan European included a TCS traction control system, to improve drive on slippery surfaces.

Low-mounted mirrors give a superb view behind and help protect the rider's hands from wind and weather. The turn signals are also built in.

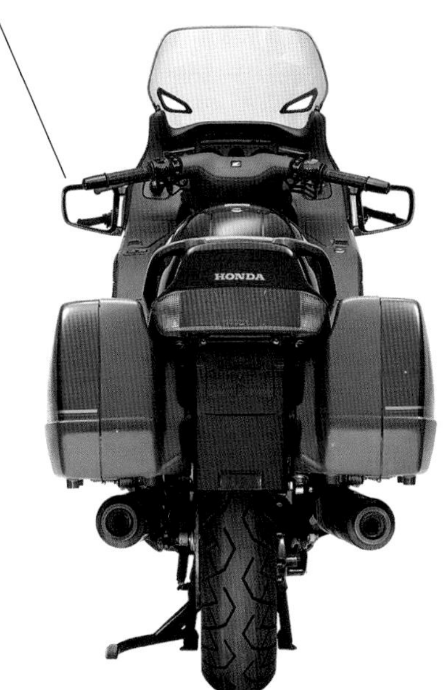

Small slats in the windscreen smooth out airflow over the rider's helmet.

A pair of steel bars either side of the fairing help protect the engine and bodywork from damage in low-speed spills. They are hidden by easily replaced black plastic covers.

The requirements for a top-class heavyweight tourer are simple – a large-capacity, flexible engine, with shaft drive, protective bodywork and a comfortable riding position are the main essentials. Ample fuel capacity, hard luggage and pillion provision are also needed, as is reliability and low maintenance.

Honda's ST1100 Pan European amply fulfils all these needs, and more. First presented in 1989, it continued at the top of the touring class for more than 12 years, until being replaced by an updated 1300cc (79ci) version in 2002.

At the heart of the Pan, and responsible for much of its success, is a 1084cc (66ci),

The right cylinder bank can clearly be seen in the stripdown shot. The transverse layout of the 90 degree V-four engine positions the carburettors and airbox above the engine, between cylinders.

16-valve, DOHC, transverse-mounted, V-four engine. Liquid-cooled, and with a five-speed gearbox and shaft final drive, the ST's engine delivers its 75kw (100bhp) in a rush of smooth, progressive thrust. Famously reliable, the ST engine is also economical, easily returning 18km/l (50mpg) fuel consumption on a tour, which in turn allows a tank range of 480km (300 miles).

COMFORT AND EASE

Matching the ST1100 Pan European's capable engine is a strong, stable chassis. The steel-tube frame is stiff, though heavy, and the conventional front forks and adjustable rear monoshock give a compliant, comfortable ride. Later Pans used linked three-piston brake calipers all round, and Honda also offered an ABS anti-lock brake equipped model.

Spacious hard panniers are supplied as standard on this model, with an optional topbox also available. The tall windscreen guides wind and rain over the rider and pillion, and the enveloping fairing also protects legs and feet from the weather. The comprehensive dashboard includes a clock, fuel gauge and trip meters, as well as a large speedometer and tachometer. Finally, a broad, comfortable dual seat supplies ample space for rider and pillion, remaining comfortable during the longest journeys.

Honda ST1100A Pan European

Top speed:	216km/h (135mph)
Engine type:	1084cc (66ci), l/c 90° V-twin, 16-valve, DOHC
Max power:	75kw (100bhp) @ 7500rpm
Frame type:	steel-tube cradle
Tyre sizes:	front 110/80 18, rear 160/70 17
Final drive:	shaft
Gearbox:	five-speed
Weight:	279kg (614lb)

JAPAN

Honda F6C Valkyrie

In a moment of audacious brilliance, Honda designers decided to build a custom cruiser version of the flat-six, 1470cc (90ci) Gold Wing. The result is the staggering F6C Valkyrie.

Cruiser styling demands plenty of chrome plating, and the Valkyrie is festooned in it, particularly the clocks, engine covers, exhaust, suspension and headlight.

The Valkyrie is named after a race of war goddesses from Norse mythology.

Six small 28mm (1.1in) CV carburettors feed the fuel/air mixture into the engine.

The triple disc brakes have unassuming twin-piston calipers and look rather feeble. But they work surprisingly well.

The twin shock rear suspension has preload adjustability for use when riding with a pillion.

A massive chrome front plate covers the silent, toothed camshaft drive belt, which runs across the front of the engine.

The heavy duty, chromed, frame-mounted engine bars are essential to prevent engine damage from small low-speed crashes or other minor collisions.

The wide machined aluminium disc-type wheels wear fat cruiser-style rubber, with a massive 150-section front tyre.

Custom cruiser motorcycles are often designed with bold, brash lines and extravagant detailing. But none is as impressive as Honda's F6C Valkyrie, based on the GL1500 Gold Wing's six-cylinder engine. This huge water-cooled, flat-six, 12-valve powerplant is festooned with chrome plate and housed in a steel-tube cruiser chassis. Wide, pullback handlebars sit atop kicked-out 43mm (1.7in) upside-down front forks, and the low, broad seat is elaborately upholstered. The transmission has five gears and a dry clutch, while final drive is by a clean, maintenance-free shaft drive.

Stripped down, the immense engine can be seen dominating the F6C, looking more like a car engine than a motorcycle powerplant. The Gold Wing's flat-six engine layout can clearly be seen on the Valkyrie.

STYLISH TOURING

While the appearance of the Valkyrie is certainly striking, it is the motorcycle's performance that is its most startling feature. Most cruiser-type machines have rather mediocre performance, particularly when it comes to handling; however, the F6C performs admirably for its size and mass. The engine's 75kw (100bhp) is delivered in a smooth, powerful surge of acceleration, and the machine's strong brakes, capable suspension and stiff frame deliver surprisingly accomplished steering precision and handling. Indeed, the main limit to spirited riding is the limited ground clearance - the Valkyrie soon starts to scrape along the ground if cornered fast.

Like the Gold Wing, which serves as the basis of the Valkyrie, there is a large range of aftermarket accessories available, allowing owners to customize their machines. Parts such as touring screens and saddlebags mean that the Valkyrie can serve as a stylish tourer. Indeed, Honda produced a factory-equipped Valkyrie Tourer for sale in the USA, which came with an official Honda windshield and weatherproof hard bags. These parts combine with the base bike's comfortable seat - especially for two-up riding - and large fuel range to make the Valkyrie an eye-catching, exotic alternative to the normal touring-class machine.

Honda F6C Valkyrie

Top speed:	200km/h (125mph)
Engine type:	1520cc (93ci), l/c flat-six, 12-valve, SOHC
Max power:	75kw (100bhp) @ 6000rpm
Frame type:	steel tube spine
Tyre sizes:	front 150/80 17, rear 180/70 16
Final drive:	shaft
Gearbox:	five-speed
Weight:	309kg (680lb)

JAPAN

JAPAN

HONDA GL1500 GOLD WING

The supertourer to beat all supertourers, Honda's massive GL1500 Gold Wing was the most luxuriously equipped motorcycle available when it first appeared in 1988.

The handlebar switches operate the sound system, cruise control and intercom, as well as the normal motorcycle functions.

An onboard electric air compressor can be used to increase pressure in the Wing's air suspension, as well as to inflate the tyres.

The twin front discs are hidden by stylish chrome disc covers. The front and rear brakes are linked: pressing the rear brake pedal also operates one front-disc caliper.

The fuel tank is mounted below the seat and holds 23l (5gal) of petrol.

The passenger is cosseted by a full backrest and wide footrests. Two speakers on the rear panels allow the pillion to hear the built-in sound system.

Vents in the windscreen and fairing allow fine-tuning of cooling or warming airflow into the rider's area.

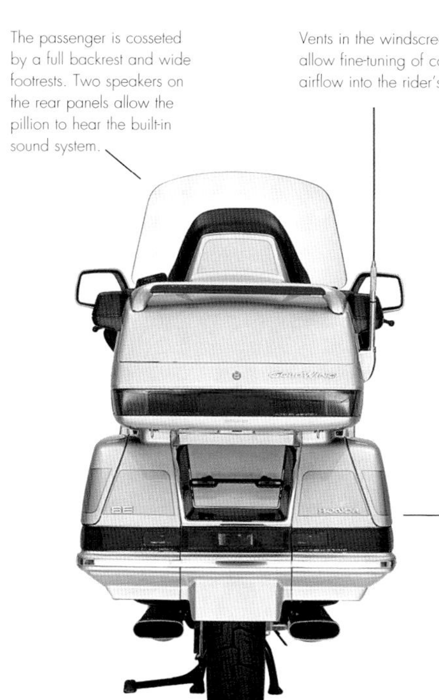

The cavernous side panniers and topbox hold huge amounts of luggage, as well as an optional CD multichanger.

The Gold Wing has defined the superheavyweight touring class since the 1100cc (67ci) four-cylinder version appeared in 1980. The earlier 999cc (61ci) version was a supersports bike, with no fairing and a shorter, more dynamic chassis.

But it was when the GL1500 appeared in 1988 that the Gold Wing really dominated motorcycle touring. Its flat six, liquid-cooled engine provided incredibly fluid, smooth power, transferred through a five-speed gearbox and shaft final drive to the rear

With most of the bodywork removed, the steel-tube perimeter frame can be seen snaking round the huge engine. The massive battery needed for the complex electrical system can also be seen below the seat.

tyre. A reverse gear helped parking and low-speed manoeuvring, and twin 33mm (1.3in) CV carburettors ensured smooth, torquey power delivery. The chassis was built around a steel-tube frame, with conventional front forks, and a twin rear shock swingarm. Disc brakes all round offered dependable stopping power, even considering the Wing's considerable 372kg (818lb) mass.

LUXURY TOURING

But it was the accommodation for rider and pillion, and the equipment levels, which really marked out the Gold Wing as a luxury supertourer. A huge, padded dual seat with built-in backrests gave superb comfort for many hundreds of miles, while the massive full fairing and tall windscreen cocooned rider and passenger in a bubble of still air and kept the weather off. Hard luggage, stereo and a fully featured dash make the Wing experience more akin to a luxury car than a motorcycle.

Riding the Gold Wing is initially an intimidating experience because of the extreme all-up weight. However, the low seat, wide bars and low centre of gravity all help slow-speed running, and the rider soon gets used to the size and weight. At normal road speeds, however, the Wing is surprisingly civilized, with no more fuss than a standard large tourer.

Honda GL1500 Gold Wing

Top speed:	192km/h (120mph)
Engine type:	1520cc (93ci), l/c flat six, 12-valve, SOHC
Max power:	75kw (100bhp) @ 5200rpm
Frame type:	steel-tube spine
Tyre sizes:	front 130/70 18, rear 160/80 16
Final drive:	shaft
Gearbox:	five-speed
Weight:	372kg (818lb)

JAPAN

Kawasaki ZXR400

Kawasaki's race-replica ZXR400 is a true 'pocket rocket' – a mini-superbike with all the performance of its larger 750cc (46ci) and 600cc (37ci) siblings, in a small-capacity package.

Two ribbed air hoses channel cool air through the fuel tank to help cool the ZXR's cylinder head.

The steel fuel tank holds 14l (3.1 gal) of unleaded petrol.

The ZXR400 is really best ridden solo. But there is a small pillion seat for occasional passengers.

The ZXR has strong, progressive front brakes, which use dual four-piston calipers and 310mm (12.2in) floating discs.

A stiff, lightweight aluminium twin-beam frame is constructed from extruded spars and cast steering head, and swingarm pivot sections welded together.

A black-finished aluminium silencer is fitted to a four-into-one steel exhaust system.

The less powerful ZXR400 uses narrower tyres than its larger capacity counterparts. A 160-section rear sports radial gives excellent grip and quick steering.

The ZXR engine is a conventional, inline-four, 16-valve design, with four 32mm (1.2in) Keihin carburettors and liquid-cooling. It was developed from the 1989 ZX-4 engine.

JAPAN

The smallest member of Kawasaki's ZXR family (with the exception of the Japan-only ZXR250), the ZXR400 is a fully equipped miniature superbike. With styling which echoes its awesome larger siblings, adjustable, track-ready suspension and a motor which screams its way right up to 14,500rpm, the ZXR400 is a superb choice for novice superbike riders.

Its high performance and specification belie its age, however: the ZXR400 first appeared in showrooms as early as 1991, as a product of the Japanese 400cc (24ci) licence limit. Taking over from earlier designs such

With the full racing fairing removed, the large water- and oil-cooling system radiators can be seen in front of the engine. The bolt-on aluminium subframe, which supports the seat unit, is also visible.

as the ZX-4 and GPZ400, the ZXR was up against stiff competition from other Japanese models, such as Honda's VFR400, Yamaha's FZR400R and Suzuki's GSX-R400. But Kawasaki's trademark strong, powerful engine design and a capable chassis put the ZXR at the top of the pile, along with the superb Honda VFR400 and CBR400.

POWER AT SPEED

Riding the ZXR is a thrilling, involved experience. The minimal weight, stiff frame and good-quality suspension give a firm yet compliant ride, which feels at home on winding back roads or tight race tracks. The liquid-cooled inline-four engine makes the most of its power higher up in the rev range, above 10,000rpm, so it is vital to keep stirring the fluid six-speed gearbox for maximum acceleration.

Ridden at a more sedate pace, the ZXR400 is less impressive. The sporty riding position puts a lot of weight through the rider's wrists, and the riding position is rather cramped. Pillion accommodation is also pretty marginal.

Many ZXR400s found their way onto race tracks around the world. Supersport 400 racing is a thriving class in many countries, and, because the ZXR is cheap and easy to tune for more power, it is very popular among club racers.

Kawasaki ZXR400

Top speed:	224km/h (140mph)
Engine type:	398cc (24ci), l/c inline-four, 16-valve, DOHC
Max power:	48kw (65bhp) @ 13,000rpm
Frame type:	aluminium twin spar
Tyre sizes:	front 120/60 17, rear 160/60 17
Final drive:	chain
Gearbox:	six-speed
Weight:	162kg (357lb)

JAPAN

Kawasaki GPZ500S

Combining commuter usefulness and everyday practicality with a sporty character, the GPZ500S is ideal for novice riders, as well as those on a tight budget.

The steel fuel tank has an 18l (3.96 gal) capacity. That's enough for more than 290km (180 miles) between stops.

The GPZ uses two 34mm (1.3in) Keihin carburettors.

Disc brakes front and rear are operated by a sliding twin-piston caliper front and a single-piston caliper rear. Later models have dual front discs.

Parallel twin engines are unusual in pure sports bikes, but they are fine for light sporty commuters. Power output is modest, but it is a very economic engine, with low fuel consumption and simple maintenance.

The GPZ500 is also known as the EX500 or Ninja 500 in different world markets.

A two-into-two painted-steel exhaust system gives a good spread of power, but is susceptible to corrosion. Aluminium silencers are fitted on each side.

Both side and centre stands are fitted to the GPZ, extending its practicality.

One of Kawasaki's longest serving models, the GPZ500S is a sporty, middleweight commuter, mixing value-for-money riding with a sporty edge. First presented in 1987 as a sporting model, the GPZ500 used a variant of the EN450 LTD custom bike's engine, itself based on half of a GPZ900R engine.

This 498cc (30ci) parallel twin engine was an advanced design in 1987, with liquid-cooling, twin overhead camshafts and four valves per cylinder. Producing 45kw (60bhp), the 500S engine was a lighter replacement for older designs such as the GPZ550. The more compact motor was installed in a simple steel-tube cradle

The simple square-section steel-tube frame can be seen traversing a straight line from the steering head to the swingarm area. The parallel twin engine is mounted in the frame's cradle rails, and the airbox is located under the seat.

frame, with a full plastic sports fairing and conventional suspension systems. The front used telescopic forks, while the rear suspension used Kawasaki's Uni-Trak monoshock setup.

SPORTY PERFORMANCE

The resulting light sportster found an immediate niche among less experienced riders who were looking for their first 'big' bike after passing their test. It also gave excellent service as a sporty commuting machine, with sufficient performance for weekend fun rides and the practical aspects necessary for daily high-mileage use.

In 1994, the GPZ500S received its only real update, which mostly focused on the chassis. The narrow 41cm (16in) wheels of the first model were replaced by wider 43cm (17in) parts, fitted with more modern sporting tyres. Stiffer handling was provided by larger diameter 37mm (1.5in) front forks, and a new rear disc brake replaced the old bike's rear drum brake. Cosmetic changes included new colours and a new, sleeker fairing design, while the seat height was lowered, to suit shorter riders.

The changes were perfect for the GPZ500S: its handling was improved, enhancing riding pleasure and performance, without altering the essential useful, economic character of the bike.

Kawasaki GPZ500S

Top speed:	209km/h (130mph)
Engine type:	498cc (30ci), l/c parallel-twin, eight-valve, DOHC
Max power:	45kw (60bhp) @ 10,000rpm
Frame type:	steel-tube double cradle
Tyre sizes:	front 110/70 17, rear 130/70 17
Final drive:	chain
Gearbox:	six-speed
Weight:	176kg (388lb)

Kawasaki KH500

Developed from the legendary H1, Kawasaki's KH500 was one of the most exciting motorcycles of the 1970s, with stunning engine performance in a rather mediocre chassis.

Early H1 versions of the 500 triple had a twin leading shoe drum front brake. Later models, such as this KH500, have a single hydraulic disc brake.

The KH500 has a total-loss lubrication system. Special two-stroke oil is pumped from a small tank below the seat and sprayed into the engine inlet tract. This oil mist lubricates the piston and conrod bearings, and is then burnt or ejected from the exhaust.

The KH500 motor was rather unreliable. The centre cylinder was prone to seizing due to insufficient cooling, and spark plugs were regularly fouled by carbon deposits.

A small hydraulic steering damper was intended to mask the serious shortcomings of the chassis, by reducing wobble and weave at high speeds. It was only partially successful.

Two-stroke engines work best with a single exhaust for each cylinder, so the KH500 has a three-into-three chromed exhaust system.

Before emissions regulations, increasing fuel costs and improved four-stroke designs rendered them largely obsolete, large air-cooled two-strokes were a sound choice for performance motorcycle designers in the early 1970s. Both Kawasaki and Suzuki developed models, but it was Kawasaki's two-stroke triple range which was the most memorable, for its combination of wayward handling and high power outputs. The firm produced various capacities, but the KH500 triple was perhaps the best compromise between engine power and chassis performance. First released as the H1 model in 1969, the KH500 was an instant hit, with incredible

The steel-tube spine frame under the tank was unable to handle the engine's power in early models. Later versions of the 500 had modified frames, for more strength and more stable handling at speed.

performance for the era. A 45kw (60bhp) engine in a 192kg (423lb) package made it one of the fastest accelerating bikes available - in a straight line at least. However, a weak frame, marginal suspension and poor brakes meant a serious mismatch between the speed and the handling. The design was further developed over the next seven years, with improved chassis and less abrupt engine performance, resulting in the KH500 in 1976.

STRICT REGULATION

The inline-triple engine was an air-cooled, piston-ported design, mounted in a steel-tube cradle-type frame. The suspension front and rear was of conventional design: the front forks were 36mm (1.4in), unadjustable, damper-rod type parts, and the twin rear shocks offered only preload adjustment for riding with a pillion.

Although the KH500 was probably the best version of the 500cc (31ci) two-stroke, it lost the character and reputation which had made it so successful when first launched. Tighter exhaust emission and sound regulations strangled the engine's output, reducing it from 45kw (60bhp) in the first H1 to 39kw (52bhp) in the last KH500. The handling was also calmed down, with improved braking, suspension and frame parts.

Kawasaki KH500

Top speed:	190km/h (118mph)
Engine type:	498cc (30ci), a/c inline-triple, two-stroke
Max power:	39kw (52bhp) @ 7000rpm
Frame type:	steel-tube cradle
Tyre sizes:	front 3.25 x 19, rear 4.00 x 18
Final drive:	chain
Gearbox:	five-speed
Weight:	192kg (423lb)

JAPAN

Kawasaki ZX-6R Ninja

Kawasaki's 600 supersport machine, the ZX-6R is an extremely high-performance machine. But it has a practical side, too, making it perfect for everyday sportsbike fans.

The pillion seat is small and high-set, but there are two grab handles to help passengers hold on at speed.

The steel fuel tank's 18l (3.96 gal) capacity permits a fuel range in excess of 260km (160 miles).

Six-piston Tokico front calipers replaced four-piston parts in1998. Kawasaki later returned to a four-piston design in 2003.

When this 1999 model was released, the engine remained a 599cc (37ci) water-cooled inline-four with 16 valves. Later versions increased capacity to 636cc (39ci).

Like all Kawasaki sports bikes, the ZX-6R feeds air to its engine through a ram-air intake system. The two slots below the headlight lead through the frame to a high-capacity airbox. At high speed, the cool, high-velocity air pushing into the box increases engine power.

A four-into-one exhaust optimizes peak power production.

A wide 170-section rear tyre handles the Ninja's high horsepower output. Later bikes used a 180-section.

In many ways, Kawasaki can be thought of as the inventor of the 600cc (37ci) supersports class: its GPZ600R of 1985 first brought water-cooled, 16-valve power and a full aerodynamic fairing to the class. That bike was developed into the GPX600 in 1988, then the ZZ-R600 in 1990; however, by the mid-1990s, a newer design was needed to compete with bikes such as Honda's CBR600 and Yamaha's FZR600R.

The ZX-6R Ninja was the result. Launched in 1995, it built on the strong engine output and stable handling of the ZZ-R600, but with more modern design, lighter weight

Stripped down, the purposeful, lightweight design is obvious. The aluminium twin-beam frame has a bolt-on subframe, and the rear monoshock piggyback reservoir is visible in front of the rear wheel.

and higher performance. A new twin-spar aluminium frame with adjustable sports suspension and dynamic full fairing housed a revised engine design, with a shorter stroke and higher rev ceiling.

SPORTING PERFORMANCE

The new bike turned out to be a revelation to ride. While not comprehensively trouncing the class-leading CBR600, the ZX-6R matched the CBR in most areas and offered an improved sporting bias. The aluminium frame was ahead of the steel-framed competition, and, even though the track performance of the new bike was superb, it was still spacious enough for two-up long-distance use.

While the first ZX-6R did not offer a massive horsepower increase over the ZZ-R, the engine had much more potential. Kawasaki increased power and torque output over the model years, with the last 599cc (37ci) ZX-6R model, the 2000–2001 J-model, offering 83kw (111bhp) in a chassis pared down to weigh just 171kg (377lb).

For 2002, Kawasaki took radical steps to improve the ZX-6R. The engine was increased in capacity to 636cc (39ci), giving it an immediate power and torque advantage. An all-new 636cc (39ci) model in 2003 put the ZX-6R firmly back on top in the intensely competitive 600 class.

Kawasaki ZX-6R Ninja

Top speed:	265km/h (165mph)
Engine type:	599cc (37ci), l/c inline-four, 16-valve, DOHC
Max power:	83kw (111bhp) @ 12,500rpm
Frame type:	aluminium twin spar
Tyre sizes:	front 120/65 17, rear 180/55 17
Final drive:	chain
Gearbox:	six-speed
Weight:	171kg (377lb)

JAPAN

Kawasaki ZZ-R600

Though introduced in 1990 as a full-on sports bike, Kawasaki's ZZ-R600 has grown old gracefully, and has been re-invented as a powerful, reliable sports-touring machine.

Early instrument panels had twin fuel warning lights, with no reserve tap. Later models had a tap, light and fuel gauge.

The single-piece seat is spacious and well padded, for long-distance comfort, even with a passenger.

Faired-in turn signals slightly improve aerodynamics and give the fairing a cleaner, smoother look.

Dual four-piston front brake calipers operate on 300mm (11.8in) semi-floating discs.

There is little remarkable about the ZZ-R's 16-valve, inline-four, water-cooled, DOHC engine, apart from impressive power and excellent reliability.

The presence of both a centre stand and a side stand makes the ZZ-R more usable as a tourer and allows easier chain and rear wheel maintenance.

Body-coloured rearview mirrors mounted on the fairing help give the ZZ-R a mature, classic style.

At high speed, the ram-air intake system produces a slight increase in intake air pressure, which increases engine output, a bit like a tiny turbocharger.

A four-into-two exhaust system boosts midrange power, enhancing the flexible nature of the ZZ-R600's power delivery.

From the early days of Japanese superbikes, Kawasaki had a reputation as a strong, powerful engine builder. The firm's ZZ-R range, released in 1990, confirmed this, both the ZZ-R1100 and this ZZ-R600 offering significantly more power than their competitors, in dynamic if slightly overweight sporting chassis. Indeed, the ZZ-R600 was powerful and sporting enough to go racing with some success: in 1990, British racer John Reynolds won the UK 600 Supercup championship.

With the aerodynamic body panels removed, the strong aluminium frame, ram-air intake system and water-cooled engine can be clearly seen.

The ZZ-R600 had a very high level of equipment and strong chassis and engine design. The 16-valve, inline-four engine was based on the firm's GPX600R design, but with extensive development to improve power, torque and reliability.

Kawasaki had also produced the first production 600 with a pressurized 'Ram-Air' system to increase power at high road speeds. This system used an air duct below the headlight to collect high-pressure air from in front of the bike, feeding it to a pressurized airbox.

CHANGING ROLES

Like the engine, the chassis was mostly a conventional design, apart from the fact that it used an aluminium frame - another first for a Japanese 600. The suspension and brakes were good-quality items, suitable for sporting road (and some track) use. Wide radial tyres meant that stickier sports tyres could be fitted.

Like several models from the early 1990s, the ZZ-R600 began life as a sports bike, but, as technology and bike design moved on, its role began to change to that of a sports tourer. Despite chassis and engine changes in 1993 and 1995 which included suspension improvements, the ZZ-R was replaced as Kawasaki's flagship 600 sports bike by the firm's more sporting ZX-6R Ninja in 1995.

Kawasaki ZZ-R600

Top speed:	249km/h (155mph)
Engine type:	599cc (37ci), l/c inline-four, 16-valve, DOHC
Max power:	73kw (98bhp) @ 12,000rpm
Frame type:	aluminium twin spar
Tyre sizes:	front 120/60 17, rear 160/60 17
Final drive:	chain
Gearbox:	six-speed
Weight:	195kg (430lb)

Kawasaki ZX-7R Ninja

One of Kawasaki's best-loved designs, the aggressively styled ZX-7R Ninja race replica brings the design and attitude of the World Superbike grid to the road.

Despite its small, uncomfortable seats and high-set pillion position, the ZX-7R has a pair of grabrails for a passenger to hold on to.

The upside-down front forks are 43mm (17in) Kayaba parts, fully adjustable for spring preload, rebound and compression damping.

Dual six-piston Tokico calipers operate on 320mm (1.2in) floating stainless-steel discs.

Kawasaki also built a ZX-7RR, the extra R denoting a race homologation model. This exotic machine was more expensive than the ZX-7R and had a single seat, power-boosting flatslide carburettors and an adjustable swingarm pivot. It also had a close-ratio racing gearbox, Nissin brakes and adjustable steering head.

The dual headlights and twin ram-air intakes give the front fairing an unmistakably aggressive profile.

A black-finished aluminium silencer and four-into-one steel exhaust system keeps noise levels low and enhances top-end power.

The Ninja was released with a super-wide 190/50 17 rear tyre. This was much wider than required by its power output and was partly a styling exercise.

Kawasaki had long placed great importance on the 750cc (46ci) class when the ZX-7R first appeared in 1996. Years of racing experience in Formula One, World Superbikes and endurance racing with the firm's ZXR750 and ZX-7R race bikes had built on the platform of successful road bikes such as the GPX750R and GPz750, so the ZX-7R had a lot to live up to.

It certainly looked the part when launched: the hunched, forward-biased fairing, endurance-style twin headlights and a pair of audacious, gaping ram-air intakes either side of the headlights gave the ZX-7R a menacing look. The chassis looked

Underneath the bright-red plastic, the ZX-7R is a largely conventional Japanese sportsbike design, with a water-cooled engine bolted into a strong aluminum frame, large airbox on top and bolt-on rear subframe.

similarly purposeful, with a racy aluminium twin-beam frame, track suspension and a massively wide 190-section rear tyre.

Hiding behind the glossy plastic flanks of the Ninja was a revised version of the firm's ZXR750 engine, which produced a creditable 91kw (122bhp). The inline-four, 16-valve, water-cooled design was unremarkable, apart from the pressurized ram-air intake system designed to increase peak power at high speeds.

MODERATE SUCCESS

The first launch reports praised the ZX-7R chassis: the front end weight bias gives very secure, confident handling, while the six-piston brake calipers and upside-down forks work well. What let the ZX-7R down, however, was its excessive weight and average peak power figure. Compared with Suzuki's GSX-R750 WT of the same year, the Kawasaki was 24kg (53lb) heavier and 5kw (7bhp) less powerful.

Unlike its peers, the ZX-7R seemed to be neglected in terms of product updates over the next seven years of its life, before being discontinued in 2002. It received no changes, apart from colour schemes, during its production life, despite Suzuki's GSX-R750 going through another two major revisions, losing 13kg (29lb) and gaining 9.7kw (13bhp) in the process.

Kawasaki ZX-7R Ninja (2000)

Top speed:	266km/h (165mph)
Engine type:	748cc (46ci), l/c inline-four, 16-valve, DOHC
Max power:	91kw (122bhp) @ 11,400rpm
Frame type:	aluminium twin spar
Tyre sizes:	front 120/70 17, rear 190/50 17
Final drive:	chain
Gearbox:	six-speed
Weight:	203kg (448lb)

Kawasaki ZX-9R Ninja

While Kawasaki's ZX-9R couldn't match the 1000cc (61ci) competition from other Japanese firms in pure racetrack performance, the power-packed 900 makes a superb, exhilarating road bike.

The steeply raked front fairing reduces aerodynamic drag at high speeds and guides the windblast up and over the rider's shoulders.

The formed steel petrol tank holds a useful 19l (4.2 gal) of unleaded fuel. There is also a reserve tap below the seat.

Despite the passenger seat and twin grabrails, the ZX-9R's extreme acceleration and powerful brakes mean the rider must take great care when carrying a pillion.

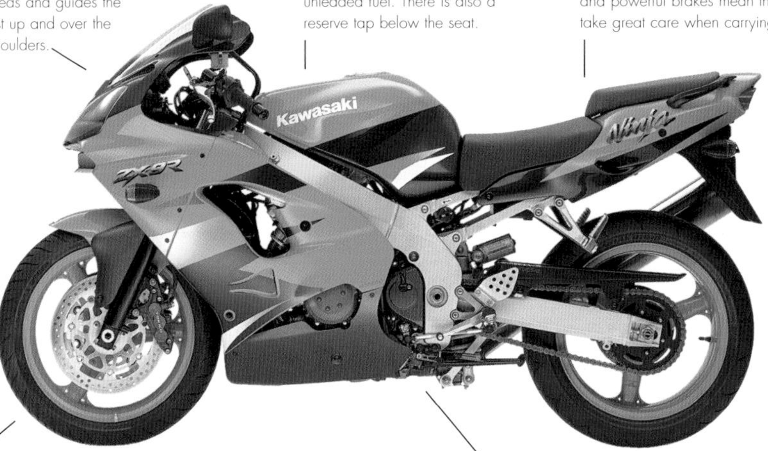

Like the firm's ZX-6R, the ZX-9R moved from four-piston front brake calipers, to six-piston calipers, then back to four-piston again. The floating stainless-steel discs on this E-model are 310mm (12.2in) in diameter.

The ZX-9R engine is a conventional design, with 16 valves, water cooling and ram-air intake.

The grey-coloured air intake snout denotes this bike as a 2000–2001 E model.

Kawasaki made the large silencer tube from light yet tough titanium, to save weight. The remaining four-into-one exhaust system is made from stainless steel.

Kawasaki's ZX-9R was the first of the new-generation ZX-R Ninja family when it appeared in 1994, a year ahead of the ZX-6R. The ZX-9R marked a return to a more sporty litre-class product from Kawasaki – its original large-capacity sporting range had developed into the heavyweight ZZ-R1100, which was more sports tourer than race replica. Honda's CBR900RR FireBlade refocused the market in 1992 towards smaller, lighter designs, and the ZX-9R was Kawasaki's response.

The first ZX-9R was unremarkable apart from its strong, powerful engine. However,

With the full race fairing removed, the rather large engine and deep aluminium frame rails can be seen. A large plastic airbox sits atop the engine, under the fuel tank.

the engine was based on the old ZXR750's motor, with a larger bore and stroke, rather than being an all-new design. The old engine and slightly flabby chassis meant the first ZX-9R was rather overweight, though: it was 30kg (66lb) heavier than the FireBlade.

Despite this, the first Kawasaki ZX-9R enjoyed some sales success, thanks in part to the bike's more practical nature - it was more suited for touring riding and had an incredibly high top speed.

A LATE CONTENDER

It was not until 1998, when Kawasaki produced an all-new engine with more oversquare architecture, and a totally new chassis to match, that the ZX-9R was on a par with Honda's FireBlade. It had shed 32kg (70lb) in weight and gained 12kw (16bhp), as well as a new WSB-derived frame, stronger brakes and better suspension.

The new bike was a genuine contender in the 1000cc (61ci) class, but, unfortunately for Kawasaki, Yamaha's R1 was launched at the same time, moving performance and handling into a new league, and knocking the FireBlade off top spot. The ZX-9R's update had come too late.

Revisions in 2000 and 2002 further improved the ZX-9R, but improved competition kept it as an also-ran in the litre sportsbike class.

Kawasaki ZX-9R Ninja (2000)

Top speed:	274km/h (170mph)
Engine type:	899cc (55ci), l/c inline-four, 16-valve, DOHC
Max power:	113kw (152bhp) @11,000rpm
Frame type:	aluminium twin spar
Tyre sizes:	front 120/70 17, rear 190/50 17
Final drive:	chain
Gearbox:	six-speed
Weight:	183kg (403lb)

JAPAN

JAPAN

Kawasaki GPZ1100

Built around a retuned engine taken from the legendary ZZ-R1100 supersports tourer, the GPZ1100 offered similar performance in a cheaper, more touring-biased package.

The front brakes are dual Tokico twin-piston calipers, biting on 300mm (1.1in) discs. Kawasaki also built an ABS version, with an anti-lock braking system, Kawasaki's only such model.

The 22l (4.8 gal) fuel tank is made of steel and is suitable for holding a magnetic-fixed tank bag.

Changes to the ZZ-R1100 engine included smaller 36mm (1.4 in) sidedraught carburettors, rather than the 40mm (1.6 in) downdraught carburettors mounted above the engine on the ZZ-R.

The capital 'Z' in the GPZ1100's name means water-cooled, while a small 'z' means air-cooled. This distinguishes the new bike from the older air-cooled GPz1100 from 1983.

The rear suspension monoshock unit is adjustable for spring preload and rebound damping.

The full fairing offers decent wind and weather protection, but has rather bland styling, looking very similar to the GPZ500S commuter model.

A four-into-two steel exhaust system is susceptible to corrosion in damp climates.

The first GPz1100 was a fire-breathing sports bike in the early 1980s, using an air-cooled four-cylinder engine in a heavyweight sporting chassis. The model name fell into disuse when Kawasaki's GPz900R replaced the 1100 design, but the designation was revived in 1995 when the GPZ1100 sports tourer was launched. The newer bike had nothing in common with the older bike apart from the name. It used a detuned version of Kawasaki's ZZ-R1100 engine in a cheap, simple chassis, in an assault on the budget sport-tourer market. The engine was modified

The GPZ1100 eschewed the aluminium frame used in the ZZ-R1100 in favour of a budget steel- tube frame. While stiff enough for touring riders, it does add weight and height to the bike.

with smaller carburettors and different camshafts to produce stronger low-down power compared with the high-horsepower ZZ-R1100. This softer power delivery is more suited to relaxed touring riding, at which the GPZ1100 is aimed.

SAFE BRAKING

A stylish, aerodynamic full fairing shares a family resemblance to Kawasaki's other GPZ models and provides excellent protection from wind and weather at high speeds. Conventional unadjustable 41mm (1.6in) front forks and a single rear Uni-Trak monoshock unit give a soft, compliant ride, ideal for absorbing bumps and ruts on long touring rides.

The combination of a powerful 92kw (123bhp) engine and a high all-up weight of over 250kg (551lb) means the GPZ1100's brakes must work hard. Twin front discs use basic but effective sliding twin-piston calipers, and an optional ABS anti-lock braking system improved safety and braking performance on slippery road surfaces.

Riding the GPZ1100 confirms the status of the machine as a very accomplished distance bike. The spacious seat is comfortable for rider and pillion, the large 22l (4.8gal) fuel tank gives an easy 325km (202 miles) between fuel stops, while optional factory-fit panniers provide ample luggage space.

Kawasaki GPZ1100

Top speed:	224km/h (140mph)
Engine type:	1052cc (64ci), l/c inline-four, 16-valve, DOHC
Max power:	92kw (123bhp) @ 9500rpm
Frame type:	steel-tube spine
Tyre sizes:	front 120/70 17, rear 170/60 17
Final drive:	chain
Gearbox:	six-speed
Weight:	242kg (534lb)

JAPAN

JAPAN

KAWASAKI ZRX1100

Despite looking like an early 1980s superbike, the ZRX1100 is a thoroughly modern sports bike. Its retro styling gives it an extra dimension, which many riders love.

The retro-styled dual seat is deeply padded and offers excellent comfort levels for rider and passenger. Dual grabrails help pillions hold on.

The front brakes do not hide their modern provenance: a pair of six-piston Tokico calipers biting on 310mm (12.2in) discs.

Kawasaki took the engine from the GPZ1100 and cosmetically enhanced it with fake cooling fins, polished camshaft cover and gloss black finished cases.

Twin rear Kayaba shocks are high-quality parts, with 'piggyback' gas-charged damping oil reservoirs. They are adjustable for spring preload, rebound and compression damping.

Classic twin clock pods hold a pair of analogue dials for speed and engine rpm, as well as indicator lights and a temperature gauge.

The square headlight, surrounded by a small plastic fairing, echoes the design cues of Kawasaki's early 1980s GPZ and Z models.

The large-capacity aluminium alloy muffler is upswept to improve ground clearance when cornering.

Over the years, Kawasaki has produced several models that celebrate the firm's heritage, from the W650 retro machine which echoes the firm's 1966 W1 model, to the 1970s-styled Zephyr range of the 1990s. But perhaps the most evocative model ever produced by the firm is the ZRX1100, which was designed to resemble Kawasaki's superbike race bikes of the early 1980s, in particular the AMA superbike championship Z1100 ridden by Eddie Lawson.

The ZRX1100 first appeared in late 1996, where its styling package of a small handlebar

Under the ZRX1100's handsome fuel tank, the heavily braced steel-tube frame cradles the four- cylinder engine. The downtubes in front of the engine are removable to help maintenance.

fairing, slab-sided fuel tank, tubular swingarm and twin rear shocks was an instant hit with press and enthusiasts alike.

MIDRANGE PERFORMER

Unlike the old air-cooled Zephyr 1100 it replaced, however, the ZRX offered a very modern performance package. Its engine was borrowed from the 1995 GPZ1100, which in turn was based upon the legendary ZZ-R1100 powerplant. Retuned with smaller carburettors and softer camshaft profiles, the ZRX engine offered a lower peak power figure of just 73kw (98bhp), compared with the 92kw (123bhp) of the GPZ or the 110kw (147bhp) of the ZZ-R. That figure belies the ZRX's strong midrange power, though, and the reshaped power curve is much more suited to an unfaired, backroads machine and its upright, unprotected riding position.

The ZRX1100 chassis is also eminently suitable for the bike's role. It is a simple design, deliberately so, in order to echo the Lawson bike, with a steel-tube cradle frame, twin-shock tubular swingarm and conventional forks. The parts are of modern design, though: the swingarm is aluminium, and the forks are cartridge-damping models.

The ZRX was further improved in 2001 by a capacity increase to 1164cc (71ci) and other detail changes, the model then being renamed ZRX1200.

Kawasaki ZRX1100

Top speed:	224km/h (140mph)
Engine type:	1052cc (64ci), l/c inline-four, 16-valve, DOHC
Max power:	73kw (98bhp) @ 8500rpm
Frame type:	steel-tube double cradle
Tyre sizes:	front 120/70 17, rear 170/60 17
Final drive:	chain
Gearbox:	five-speed
Weight:	222kg (488lb)

JAPAN

Kawasaki ZZ-R1100

With a heritage of fast, powerful machines behind it, Kawasaki's ZZ-R1100 had much to live up to when launched. It did just that – and more – for much of the 1990s.

Minimizing drag is as important as brute horsepower for going fast, so Kawasaki developed a very slippery, all-enveloping full fairing to cut through the air more easily.

Neat touches, such as the chromed flip-out luggage hooks, dual helmet locks and passenger grabrail, make long distance travel easy on the ZZ-R.

Both side and centre stands are fitted.

The mild steel exhaust system has a black protective finish, but can succumb to corrosion in poor climates. The large-capacity silencers have a polished stainless construction.

Kawasaki's ram-air system involves two ports below the headlight, leading to a large sealed airbox. At the speeds (275km/170mph) that the Kawasaki can achieve, this offers a small but significant power gain.

Like the ZZ-R600, the ZZ-R1100 has its front and rear turn signals blended into the main bodywork, to reduce drag.

The extreme power and weight of the ZZ-R1100 means it can wear out its wide 180-section rear tyre very quickly.

There has always been an interest in the fastest, most powerful production motorcycle, with accompanying kudos for its manufacturer. Of all the motorcycling firms in the last three decades of the twentieth century, Kawasaki managed this achievement more than most. Machines such as the Z1, GPZ900R and ZX-10 all held the title of 'world's fastest bike' at one time.

But it was the ZZ-R1100 (ZX-11 in the USA) that held the title longest, from its launch in 1990 until Honda's Super Blackbird bested it in 1997. Developed from

Removing the sleek bodywork reveals the ZZ-R1100's Y-shaped aluminium frame beams, with unboltable cradle rails, and the large engine with a massive airbox mounted above it.

the ZX-10, the ZZ-R1100 was an advanced, powerful motorcycle design which amazed the world at its launch.

The ZZ-R11 was powered by an inline-four, water-cooled, 16-valve engine based on the ZX-10 unit. But Kawasaki had refined its internals and developed a ram-air pressurized air intake system, which increases engine power at high vehicle speeds. The resulting 110kw (147bhp) powerplant was fitted in a heavyweight chassis, with an aluminium twin-spar frame and conventional running gear.

EXTREME SPEED

On the road, the ZZ-R was breathtaking. The supremely powerful engine carried bike and rider along on a relentless wave of acceleration, from any revs, in any of its six gears. Even with a passenger and luggage, which it was well suited to carrying, the ZZ-R was almost insanely fast and offered a superb way of covering many miles at great speed in relative comfort. The aerodynamic full fairing, comfy dual seat and relaxed riding position all contrast with the extreme performance.

Even when the Blackbird, and later Suzuki's Hayabusa, surpassed the ZZ-R's performance, the strong loyalty to the machine encouraged Kawasaki to update it with a 1164cc (71ci) engine and a more touring bias, and call it the ZZ-R1200.

Kawasaki ZZ-R1100

Top speed:	275km/h (171mph)
Engine type:	1052cc (64ci), l/c inline-four, 16-valve, DOHC
Max power:	110kw (147bhp) @ 10,500rpm
Frame type:	aluminium twin spar
Tyre sizes:	front 120/70 17, rear 180/55 17
Final drive:	chain
Gearbox:	six-speed
Weight:	233kg (514lb)

Kawasaki VN1500 Drifter

Taking retro design fashion to new levels, Kawasaki went back to the 1940s for inspiration for the Drifter, which is styled like the Indian motorcycle from America.

The round, chrome, 'pancake'-style air-filter case hides a modern airbox design.

The electronic fuel injection system uses twin 36mm (1.4in) throttle bodies.

The rider's seat is extremely low, allowing even the shortest rider to put both feet firmly on the floor. The passenger sits higher and has a large grabrail to hang on to.

The ignition switch is located below the fuel tank.

Wire spoked wheels with chromed rims wear wide, cruiser-style tyres.

The brakes use twin-piston calipers front and rear, and are rather marginal in terms of stopping power, particularly the single front disc.

Kawasaki also built an 800cc (49ci) version of the Drifter, with chain drive and similar styling.

The Drifter's broad seat and wide handlebars are comfortable, but the riding position is less so, particularly at higher speeds.

The rear mudguard is mounted to the swingarm to ensure constant clearance between tyre and fender, and give the necessary vintage styling.

From the appearance of Kawasaki's VN1500 Drifter, it seems more like a motorcycle launched in the early part of the 20th century, rather than one first presented in the last year of that century. That's because the Drifter is deliberately designed to look like an American cruiser motorcycle of the 1940s, the Indian. The flared mudguards, wide handlebars and long exhaust pipe, which all look so strange today, are based on the extravagant Indian design cues.

Below the unusual design, the Drifter is mostly comprised of standard cruiser parts, mainly taken from Kawasaki's VN1500 range. The engine is the venerable SOHC

With the fuel tank and seat removed, there is little of the Drifter to see apart from the huge V-twin engine and skinny steel frame tubes.

1470cc (90ci), eight-valve V-twin first used in the 1988 VN1500. Despite its age, this engine is comparatively high-tech, with twin spark plugs per cylinder head, electronic fuel injection and water-cooling.

The huge engine's considerable torque is transmitted to the wide rear tyre by a five-speed gearbox and an efficient, maintenance-free shaft drive.

HIGHWAY CRUISING

On the road, the Drifter provides the typical cruising machine experience: plenty of low-rpm pulling power, but with minimal top-end power. The engine has been tuned for torque, which allows relaxing progress with few gearchanges - the rider can essentially stay in top gear for most of the time.

Intended for American highway cruising, the Drifter was not really designed for cornering. There is little ground clearance, and it is easy to scrape the generous footboards on the ground mid-corner. Similarly, the chassis has been designed for comfort and style, so the suspension is soft front and rear, and the steel tube frame only just copes with the forces put through it by the 304kg (670lb) bulk of the Drifter.

The Drifter's broad seat and wide handlebars are comfortable, but the riding position is less so, particularly at higher speeds this machine can achieve.

Kawasaki VN1500 Drifter

Top speed:	185km/h (115mph)
Engine type:	1470cc (90ci), l/c V-twin, eight-valve, SOHC
Max power:	48kw (65bhp) @ 4700rpm
Frame type:	steel-tube cradle
Tyre sizes:	front 130/90 16, rear 150/80 16
Final drive:	shaft
Gearbox:	five-speed
Weight:	304kg (670lb)

KTM Duke 620

Based on its championship-winning offroad machines, KTM's Duke combines dirtbike power and chassis technology with superbike tyres and brakes in a strong 'supermotard' package.

The Duke is not a very practical machine. The fuel range is around 145km (90 miles), and the seat is thin and hard.

The exhaust system is made from resilient stainless steel, with a large-capacity high-mounted silencer. There are two exhaust pipes from the cylinder head, one from each exhaust valve port.

The single-cylinder engine has four valves and a single overhead camshaft. The valves are operated by roller bearing rocker arms. Carburation is by a 40mm (1.5in) Dell'Orto carburettor, and a single balancer shaft reduces vibration.

A close-fitting rear 'hugger' mudguard protects the rear shock and engine from splashes from the rear tyre.

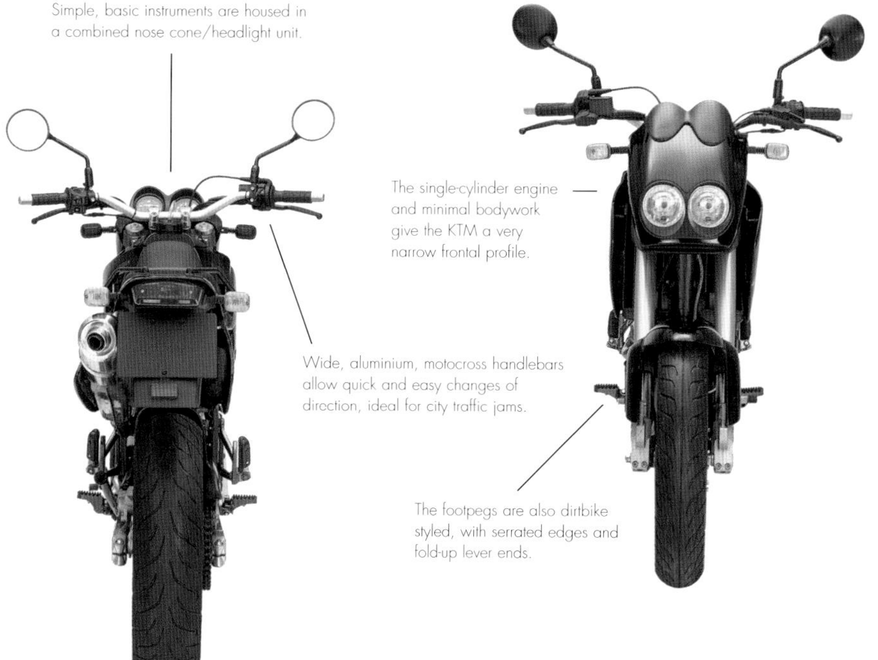
Simple, basic instruments are housed in a combined nose cone/headlight unit.
The single-cylinder engine and minimal bodywork give the KTM a very narrow frontal profile.
Wide, aluminium, motocross handlebars allow quick and easy changes of direction, ideal for city traffic jams.
The footpegs are also dirtbike styled, with serrated edges and fold-up lever ends.

Austrian firm KTM (named after the initials of the founders and the town where the company began) began in the 1950s, producing off-road motorcycles. But in 1994 it unveiled a different machine to the enduro and motocross competition machines for which it was known. The KTM Duke was a new type of motorcycle, described as a 'supermotard' or 'dual-sport' machine. In essence, a supermotard is a dirt bike fitted with wheels, tyres and brakes more suited to Tarmac use than dirt use.

The Duke was built around KTM's single-cylinder, water-cooled, four-stroke, 609cc

Under the tank and body panels, the KTM's dirtbike-type cradle frame can be seen. This design is very tough, while remaining acceptably light and stiff.

(37ci) engine and a simple dirtbike chassis: steel tube frame, WP long-travel upside-down front forks and a WP monoshock, both fully adjustable.

But the dirtbike parts list stopped at the wire-spoked wheel hubs. The wheel rims are 43cm (17in) parts, wearing sticky road tyres, and the front wheel wears a large, 320mm (12.2in) floating brake disc with a four-piston Brembo caliper. A neat nose cone holds two headlights and keeps some windblast off the rider.

STUNT RIDER

This lightweight, minimalistic machine excels at sub-160km/h (100mph) mountain road riding or battling through urban sprawl. That single-cylinder engine provides a mighty dose of low-down grunt, providing addictive acceleration out of every corner, while the high-specification chassis components let the rider get the absolute best from the engine's 41kw (55bhp). Like most other supermotards, the Duke is an excellent stunt machine – the light weight, strong brakes and grunty engine allowing wheelies and stoppies at the drop of a hat.

In 1998, KTM updated the Duke to the Duke II model with a bigger 624cc (38ci) engine, aluminium wheels and twin underseat silencers.

KTM Duke 620

Top speed:	170km/h (105mph)
Engine type:	624cc (38ci), l/c single cylinder, four-valve, SOHC
Max power:	41kw (55bhp) @ 7250rpm
Frame type:	Chrome-moly steel-tube double cradle
Tyre sizes:	front 120/70 17, rear 160/60 17
Final drive:	chain
Gearbox:	five-speed
Weight:	145kg (320lb)

AUSTRIA

ITALY

Laverda 750S Formula

The 750S Formula is a special high-power version of the firm's basic 750S. With extra power and higher quality chassis components, it is an accomplished Italian sports bike.

The Formula's fuel injection is an uprated Weber Marelli system.

The rear shock is fully adjustable and has a remote reservoir, mounted below the seat. This reservoir helps keep the damping oil cooler under hard use.

The Brembo brakes are top-specification four-piston calipers and dual 320mm (1.3in) floating discs.

The six-speed gearbox is an elderly design and rather clunky.

The premium chassis components include these lightweight Marchesini wheels, shod with sticky Pirelli sports tyres.

The two air ducts in the front fairing feed cooling air into the airbox, boosting power at high speed and reducing power losses associated with breathing air warmed by the engine.

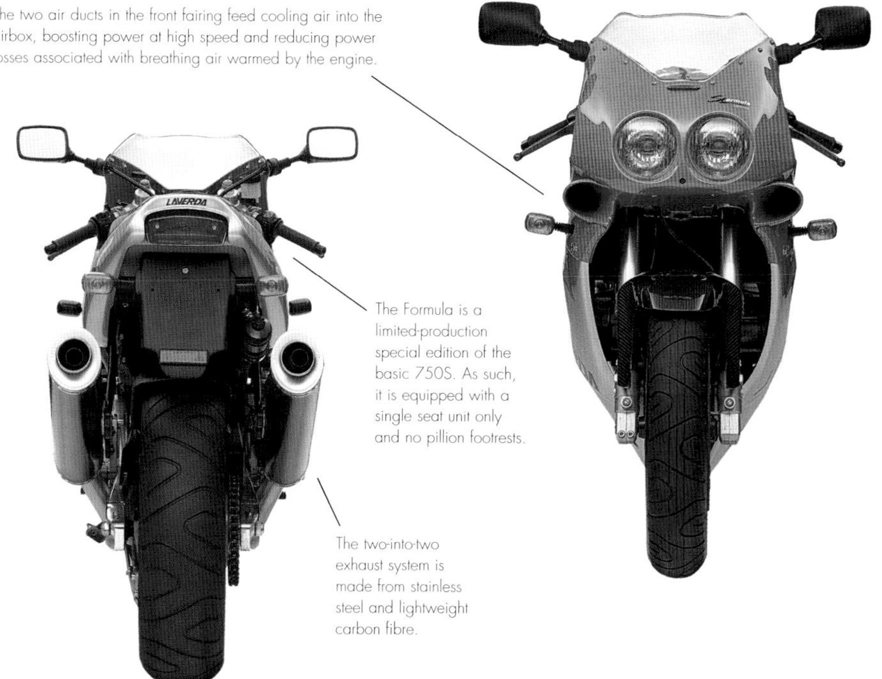

The Formula is a limited-production special edition of the basic 750S. As such, it is equipped with a single seat unit only and no pillion footrests.

The two-into-two exhaust system is made from stainless steel and lightweight carbon fibre.

Laverda was one of the most famous names in Italian motorcycling from the years after World War II and right up to the 1970s. This was thanks to machines such as the legendary Jota three-cylinder superbike and the 750SFC. But the firm fell on hard times in the late 1980s, and production almost stopped entirely.

Then, in the early 1990s, the firm released a new sportsbike range, based on its elderly 500cc (31ci) parallel twin engine from the Alpina/Montjuic model. The firm lacked the resources to develop an all-new engine, but it updated the design with different ancillaries and top-end revisions in an attempt to modernize its performance. So

Below the fairing, the Formula is dominated by a massive airbox mounted above the engine. The fuel tank is actually located below the rear seat unit; the filler cap is under the seat cover.

an electronic fuel injection system replaced the carburettors; the capacity increased to 668cc (41ci), then 748cc (46ci); and first oil- and then water-cooling systems were added.

The resulting 750 engine was the last evolution of the Montjuic engine, and it is this unit which powers the 750S Formula, a special limited-edition version of the standard 750S. Despite its ancient foundations, the motor produces respectable peak power, although the power delivery is rather revvy and harsh.

PRECISION HANDLING

In contrast to the engine, the Formula chassis is thoroughly modern. A stiff aluminium twin-spar frame is the match of anything produced by Japan, while high-quality chassis components festoon the bike. Fully adjustable Paioli upside-down racing forks and rear monoshock and Brembo brakes are among the finest components available, and it was these that helped give the Formula precise, fine handling on both road and track.

The Formula was a worthy competitor to Ducati's 748 Superbike and an interesting alternative to mainstream Japanese 600s. But questionable reliability and build quality dogged production, and financial woes were never far away. Eventually, at the beginning of 2001, Laverda was sold to Aprilia.

Laverda 750S Formula

Top speed:	242km/h (150mph)
Engine type:	748cc (46ci), l/c parallel twin, eight-valve, DOHC
Max power:	69kw (92bhp) @ 9000rpm
Frame type:	aluminium twin spar
Tyre sizes:	front 120/60 17, rear 160/60 17
Final drive:	chain
Gearbox:	six-speed
Weight:	187kg (411lb)

Moto Guzzi California Special

Marrying classic Italian power with custom styling, the Moto Guzzi California Special is a laid-back cruising machine. It's the perfect European alternative to a Harley-Davidson.

The side-mounted hydraulic steering damper is fitted between the forks and the frame to reduce steering wobble and weave at higher speeds.

Unlike most modern motorcycles, the Guzzi engine operates its valves with pushrods, the camshaft being mounted low down in the engine. Harley-Davidson is the only other firm still regularly using pushrod engines.

Dual Brembo four-piston calipers and 320mm (12.5in) floating discs are a very effective braking setup.

The Guzzi engine layout is ideal for a shaft final drive setup, as the crankshaft is in line with the final drive, and there is no need for a complex bevel gearbox to turn the drive through 90°.

White-face instrument dials add a classy feel to the dashboard. The clocks themselves are basic items, with only the essential functions included.

The V-twin's air-cooled cylinder heads are ideally located, protruding into the passing airflow.

The adjustable 45mm (1.7in) Marzocchi front forks have a surprisingly high specification.

Compared with modern Japanese motorcycle manufacturers, firms such as Moto Guzzi have a much slower turnover of models and technology. But the California model is a long-running one even for Guzzi: the model name dates back to the 850 California of 1972, and the basic layout of the bike has changed very little in the three decades since.

The heart of the California Special is, like all modern Moto Guzzis, a transverse-mounted 90° air-cooled V-twin engine with shaft drive and fuel injection. The 1064cc (65ci) unit produces a rather sedate

With the fuel tank, seat and side panels taken off, the California's skinny steel-tube frame is exposed. Though insubstantial, it is adequate for the bike's gentle cruising character.

55kw (74bhp), offering a relaxed, torquey power delivery.

This engine is perfectly suited to the California's gentle cruising character. Styled like an American highway machine, it has a unique Italian flavour. A low-slung seat, pullback handlebars and low footpegs gives a relaxed riding position, while a dash of chrome plating on the engine and chassis lends a classic air to the styling.

SIMPLE TECHNOLOGY

The California's chassis is as low-tech as the engine. A steel-tube cradle frame, twin rear shocks and conventional front forks offer sufficient stiffness and wheel control for acceptable handling, although there is insufficient ground clearance on the California for committed cornering.

But like the engine, the Special's chassis does have some refinements: the front forks and shocks have adjustable damping, and the triple brake discs are linked front and rear by a proportional delay valve, to improve braking control.

The California Special was launched in 1998, then replaced in 2001 by the California Special Sport, with mostly cosmetic updates. By this time, Aprilia had taken over Moto Guzzi and begun a programme of investment and improvements in build quality.

Moto Guzzi California Special

Top speed:	198km/h (124mph)
Engine type:	1064cc (65ci), a/c 90° transverse V-twin, four-valve, OHV
Max power:	55kw (74bhp) @ 6400rpm
Frame type:	steel-tube double cradle
Tyre sizes:	front 110/90 18, rear 140/80 17
Final drive:	shaft
Gearbox:	five-speed
Weight:	251kg (553lb)

JAPAN

SUZUKI RGV250

One of the highest specification mini-superbikes ever built, Suzuki's RGV250 brought the styling and technology of the 250cc (15ci) GP grid to the streetbike world.

The RGV engine is a 90° V-twin two-stroke, with the front cylinder rotated forward. The cylinders have a tough, low-friction ceramic coating.

The RGV uses 34mm (1.3in) Mikuni carburettors with electronic variable jetting, to improve power delivery.

Opposed four-piston Tokico brake calipers bite on 300mm (11.8 in) discs. These have tangential grooves, to improve disc cooling and performance.

A duct in the fairing side panel feeds cool air to the large airbox, which is located under the fuel tank.

The RGV's guillotine-type power valves alter the characteristics of the engine's exhaust ports, allowing both strong low-down power and ultimate peak power, too. They can wear on high-mileage engines, damaging the piston.

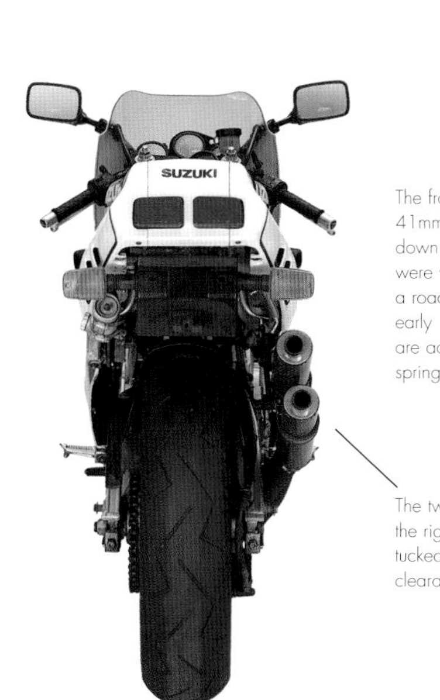

The front forks are stiff 41mm (16in) upside-down parts, which were very unusual on a road bike in the early 1990s. They are adjustable for spring preload.

The twin silencers mounted on the right-hand side are tightly tucked in to improve ground clearance during fast cornering.

JAPAN

The 250cc (15ci) sportsbike class is noteworthy for two reasons: it is an important racing class at both GP level and entry-level club racing. But it has also been an important entry level class for road bike sales, particularly in Japan. Licence laws there used to restrict riders to 250cc (15ci) and 400cc (24ci) machines, unless they had passed an advanced riding test.

These circumstances ensured that all the Japanese manufacturers produced very high specification 250cc (15ci) race-replica

Under the race-replica plastic bodywork, the massive, black expansion chamber exhaust pipes dominate, together with the huge aluminium frame beams and braced gull-wing swingarm.

machines in the early 1990s. Suzuki's RGV250 was one of the best of these machines, and it enjoyed great sales success, especially in the UK.

RACING DESIGN

The Suzuki RGV250 was a ground-up revamp of the RG250, using a 90 degree V-twin two-stroke engine mounted in a race-ready twin-beam aluminium frame. Chassis components were straight from the race track and radical for 1989: upside-down forks, gull-arm swingarm, dual four-piston front brake calipers. As for the engine, it was an extremely advanced design, with ceramic-coated cylinders, electronically controlled carburettors and electronic power valves. Large-capacity expansion chambers further optimized power, and these chambers were cunningly designed to fit under the bike, retaining good ground clearance.

The RGV is an involving machine to ride - the six-speed gearbox must be constantly stirred to keep the engine in the narrow rev range where peak power is produced. Steering is exceptionally fast, as you would expect from a 139kg (306lb) machine with a 1380mm (54in) wheelbase.

But on a track, the RGV is sublime, the strong brakes, light weight and frenetic power delivery combining to produce an intense cornering experience.

Suzuki RGV250

Top speed:	209km/h (130mph)
Engine type:	249cc (15ci), l/c 90° V-twin, two-stroke
Max power:	48kw (65bhp) @ 10,500rpm
Frame type:	aluminium twin spar
Tyre sizes:	front 110/70 17, rear 150/60 17
Final drive:	chain
Gearbox:	six-speed
Weight:	139kg (306lb)

JAPAN

Suzuki RG500

The best of the 500 Grand Prix replicas of the early 1980s, Suzuki's RG500 two-stroke is the closest to a road-going GP bike ever produced.

A large cast box behind the steering head stiffens the frame, while also holding the air filter and acting as an airbox.

The 'Deca-piston' brake setup uses twin four-piston front calipers and a single dual-piston rear caliper to make 10 pistons in total – hence the name.

The square-four design is basically two parallel twin engines, with two crankshafts, geared together. This is extremely rare on road bikes, Ariel's 1950's classic being the only other production machine to use one.

The RG500 has a very utilitarian, race-type dashboard, with just a speedometer, tachometer, engine temperature gauge and minimal warning lights mounted in a lightweight foam plate.

The RG's tyres are narrow, crossply items, with a 110-section front and a 120-section rear.

The 38mm (1.5in) front forks had small control knobs on the bottom, which adjusted a very basic anti-dive damping control mechanism, called Posi-Damp.

If any bike can be described as legendary, then Suzuki's RG500 is probably it. Even in the early part of the twenty-first century, no other production bike has been built which so closely mimics the full-bore 500cc (31ci) class of Grand Prix bike. The RG500 shared its name, engine layout, chassis design and appearance with the 500cc (31ci) GP bike raced by Suzuki from the late 1970s to the mid-1990s. The road bike obviously had less power and a road bike chassis, but was still a unique machine.

Best seen with the bodywork removed, the RG500 has two exhaust pipes running back underneath the engine from the front cylinders, and two running back under the seat from the rear cylinders. Two-stroke engines work best with one exhaust pipe per cylinder.

The RG500's 498cc two-stroke engine is powerful and compact, with a rather unusual square-four layout. The intake system is a disc valve design, where slotted metal discs on the end of the crankshafts open and close the inlet port. These slots allow the engine to draw in the fuel and air mixture from side-mounted Mikuni carburettors. This system is perhaps the optimum intake arrangement for a square-four two-stroke, but it does compromise airbox and carburettor design and is susceptible to crash damage.

RADICAL DESIGN

The radical engine package is matched to a chassis equally as radical in 1985. The frame is an aluminium square-tube cradle arrangement, with an aluminium box-section monoshock swingarm and air-adjustable front forks. Like the rest of the chassis, the brakes were excellent in 1985, but have been overtaken by modern sports components.

If the RG500's technology and design was amazing, its styling was just as impressive and still looks purposeful almost 20 years later. The twin underseat silencers were straight from the GP grid, and the aerodynamic full fairing echoed the renowned race bikes ridden by legends such as Franco Uncini, Marco Lucchinelli and Barry Sheene.

Suzuki RG500

Top speed:	217km/h (135mph)
Engine type:	498cc (30ci), l/c square four, two-stroke
Max power:	71kw (95bhp) @ 9500rpm
Frame type:	aluminium double cradle
Tyre sizes:	front 110/90 16, rear 120/90 17
Final drive:	chain
Gearbox:	six-speed
Weight:	154kg (339lb)

Suzuki GSF600 Bandit

Introduced as a budget roadster, the Bandit 600 turned out to be a huge sales success, which created a whole new class of practical, stylish high-performance middleweights.

A shapely steel fuel tank holds 19l (4.2 gal) which allows around 275km (170 miles) before a refill. The fuel reserve is operated by a tap.

The well-padded dual seat is spacious enough for long-distance touring trips, even with a passenger.

The Bandit's oil-cooled engine is an inline-four, 16-valve DOHC design, producing 58kw (78bhp). It was first used in the GSX600F sports tourer in 1988.

Rather than fit a retro-styled twin shock rear suspension unit, Suzuki used a modern aluminium swingarm with a preload adjustable monoshock unit.

The basic twin clocks are mounted in chromed pods and fitted to the handlebars. Later models had a more comprehensive dashboard mounted on the fairing.

The small frame-mounted fairing and windscreen extends the Bandit's usability, by reducing windblast at higher speeds and improving weather protection.

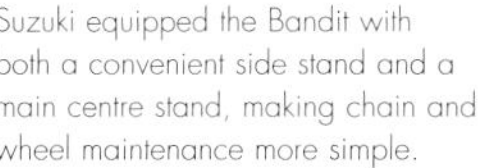

Suzuki equipped the Bandit with both a convenient side stand and a main centre stand, making chain and wheel maintenance more simple.

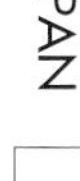

Every so often, a machine comes along which defines a new class all by itself. The Suzuki Bandit 600 is just such a bike. Launched in 1995 with minimal fanfare, the 600 Bandit seemed to be an unremarkable machine: a straightforward roadster design, with budget components mostly borrowed from existing models.

But the Bandit has two advantages: traditional styling and a very competitive price. At less than £4000 ($6000), it was just two-thirds the price of a typical 600cc (37ci)

The Bandit's round steel- tube cradle frame is cheap to fabricate, yet offers good stiffness and strength. Bracing around the steering head further improves handling.

sports bike. The budget price was possible because the Bandit used tried and tested technology. The engine was taken from the GSX600F sports tourer, which was first released in 1988, and so was very reliable, and this meant little development costs for the new bike.

RIVAL MODELS

The Bandit's chassis also managed to combine sound performance with low cost. The suspension and braking systems were budget parts, shared with other bikes in Suzuki's range, but performed well. The faired Bandit 600 pictured, the GSF600S, was launched in 1996 with a small half-fairing, making it more suitable for high-speed use.

Initially, there were no competitors for the 600 Bandit – Yamaha's Diversion was a similar bike, but offered less performance for greater expense. But after the launch of the Bandit, Honda's Hornet 600 and Yamaha's Fazer 600 copied the Bandit concept and improved upon it with modern, powerful water-cooled engines.

Suzuki revamped the Bandit in 2000 with both chassis and engine refinements. The result was a better bike, but the lack of fundamental redesign meant the Bandit remained some way behind the competition in this budget 600 roadster class that it had itself invented.

Suzuki GSF600 Bandit

Top speed:	217km/h (135mph)
Engine type:	599cc (37ci), a/c inline-four, 16-valve, DOHC
Max power:	58kw (78bhp) @ 10,500rpm
Frame type:	steel-tube double cradle
Tyre sizes:	front 120/60 17, rear 160/60 17
Final drive:	chain
Gearbox:	six-speed
Weight:	208kg (459lb)

JAPAN

Suzuki GSX-R600

A relative newcomer to the modern 600cc (37ci) sportsbike scene, Suzuki's GSX-R600 was the most extreme track-ready sports 600 available when launched in 1997.

The engine was heavily based on the GSX-R750, with a smaller bore and shorter stroke.

The brakes also distinguish between the GSX-R600 and 750 models. The 600 had four-piston Tokico calipers, while the 750 used six-piston parts.

Light three-spoke cast aluminum wheels are fitted with radial sports tyres. The rear is a wide 180/55 size – two sizes up from the smaller 160-section used by competing 600s in 1997.

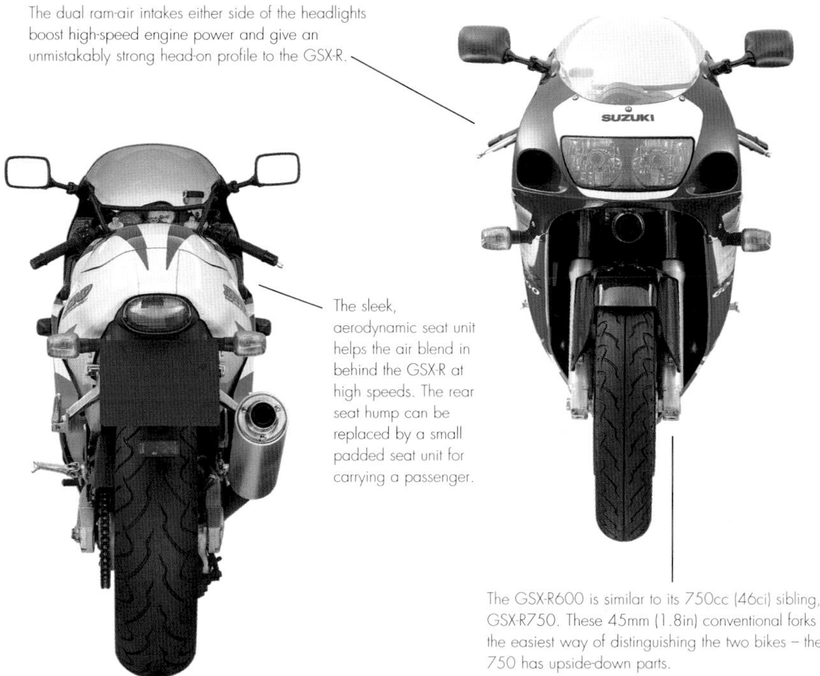

The dual ram-air intakes either side of the headlights boost high-speed engine power and give an unmistakably strong head-on profile to the GSX-R.

The sleek, aerodynamic seat unit helps the air blend in behind the GSX-R at high speeds. The rear seat hump can be replaced by a small padded seat unit for carrying a passenger.

The GSX-R600 is similar to its 750cc (46ci) sibling, the GSX-R750. These 45mm (1.8in) conventional forks are the easiest way of distinguishing the two bikes – the 750 has upside-down parts.

Although the 600cc (37ci) sportsbike class was vital for most mainstream manufacturers, Suzuki had fallen behind the competition by the mid-1990s. Its RF600 was an advanced design and a sound sports tourer, but it lacked the track performance of some of its competitors. Suzuki sold an unimpressive GSX-R600 in America in 1992, which was essentially a sleeved-down GSX-R750W. But, in 1997, the firm released a new-generation GSX-R600, similar to the SRAD GSX-R750 released the

Once the seat unit, fuel tank and full fairing are removed, the GSX-R's essentials are laid bare – a large airbox, stiff aluminium frame and compact, powerful engine unit.

year before. An unashamed race-replica track machine, the new GSX-R600 impressed with its high-revving, powerful four-cylinder four-stroke engine, stiff aluminium beam frame and fully adjustable race-specification suspension and brakes.

RACING PROWESS

Like its 750cc (46ci) sibling, the GSX-R600 was at its best when ridden on a race track. The 599cc (37ci) inline-four 16-valve engine made much of its 79kw (106bhp) high up in the rev range, and constant gearchanges were needed to keep the engine revving in its strongest power. Like the engine, the chassis was focused and committed: the riding position put the rider into an aggressive racing crouch, and a firm suspension gave precise feedback from its sticky radial tyres. There was little space for a pillion once the aerodynamic 'duck-tail' rear seat cover was removed, and the dashboard sported minimalist, racing-style instruments.

A minor update in 1998 further improved power and increased the engine's midrange drive, although Yamaha's R6 had stolen the GSX-R's performance crown. But a more fundamental revamp in 2001 put the GSX-R600 back on top, with a more powerful fuel-injected engine mounted in a cutting-edge sports chassis, based heavily on the successful GSX-R750Y of 2000.

Suzuki GSX-R600

Top speed:	266km/h (165mph)
Engine type:	599cc, l/c inline-four, 16-valve, DOHC
Max power:	79kw (106bhp) @12,000rpm
Frame type:	aluminium twin spar
Tyre sizes:	front 120/70 17, rear 180/55 17
Final drive:	chain
Gearbox:	six-speed
Weight:	174kg (383lb)

JAPAN

Suzuki SV650S

Rather than use a familiar four-cylinder layout, Suzuki chose a V-twin engine for its SV650 middleweight. The result is a sparkling performer which is packed with character.

The fuel tank holds just 16l (3.5 gal) of petrol, but the SV's reasonable fuel consumption allows a fuel range of 225km (140 miles).

While the small pillion seat is set rather high, there is a comfortable grabrail and sufficient padding for moderate touring trips.

One place where Suzuki saved money was in the brakes, which use dual-piston sliding calipers, rather than more expensive four-piston parts.

The engine was an all-new unit, developed especially for the SV. It is a reliable, powerful unit, with a strong spread of torque. The design is similar to the TL1000 unit, although the 650 uses twin 39mm (1.5in) Mikuni carburettors. From 2002, the engine was fuel-injected.

The clear, simple dashboard is mounted inside the fairing.

The wide-set rearview mirrors give a clear view of the road behind.

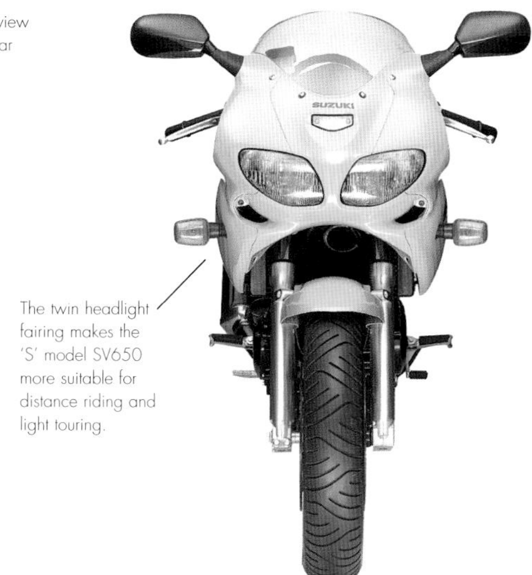

The twin headlight fairing makes the 'S' model SV650 more suitable for distance riding and light touring.

When Suzuki was preparing to launch the SV650, most observers expected the new bike to be a replacement for the firm's long-running Bandit 600 roadster. When the SV650 was finally revealed at the Milan show in 1998, however, it turned out to be slightly different from what was expected. Rather than a cheap budget bike, built to a price with parts borrowed from other bikes, the SV turned out to be a handsome, well-specified middleweight roadster.

With an aluminium trellis-type frame, sharp and modern styling and a punchy

Stripped down, the SV650 looks nothing like a budget machine. The handsome trellis aluminum frame, bolt-on subframe and compact water-cooled engine would not look out of place on a premium sports bike.

V-twin engine, the SV promised a touch more sparkle than the basic Bandit had offered. Indeed, the Bandit continued in production alongside the SV, getting its own update in 2000, confirming the different intents for both bikes.

ADVANCES ON A BUDGET

The heart of the SV is that 90° V-twin engine, developed solely for the new bike. It is an advanced design, featuring water-cooling, quad camshafts and four valves per cylinder, and it produces a healthy 52kw (70bhp). The aluminium frame is also all-new and combines sportsbike-type stiffness with light weight and stylish design. The SV650 is a budget design, though, and this shows in the chassis components. The suspension is rather basic - the 41mm (1.6in) forks are unadjustable conventional parts, and the rear monoshock is adjustable for preload only.

Despite the budget chassis, the Suzuki SV650 is a fun bike to ride. The engine delivers punchy power, while the light weight and sharp steering make it highly manoeuvrable, both desirable attributes when it comes to city riding.

Suzuki also produced an unfaired version of the SV650. It has slightly lower gearing and different instruments, as well as a more upright riding position, with straight handlebars and lower footpegs.

Suzuki SV650S

Top speed:	201km/h (125mph)
Engine type:	645cc (39ci), l/c 90° V-twin, eight-valve, DOHC
Max power:	52kw (70bhp) @ 9000rpm
Frame type:	aluminium trellis
Tyre sizes:	front 120/60 17, rear 160/60 17
Final drive:	chain
Gearbox:	six-speed
Weight:	169kg (373lb)

Suzuki GSX-R750

Perhaps the definitive Japanese sports bike, Suzuki's GSX-R750 has been battling at the top of the race-replica class since 1985, with its super blend of performance and handling.

A small hydraulic steering damper is fitted in front of the steering head, to reduce steering instability under acceleration. It can make the steering feel rather heavy at slow speeds.

The fuel injection system fitted to the GSX-R750 was rather simple compared with later versions. It is effective, though, curing the hesitations and carb-icing problems of earlier carburetted bikes.

This engine is the second-generation water-cooled engine. It features ceramic-coated cylinder bores to reduce friction and wear, straight inlet ports and light magnesium engine covers.

The T-model GSX-R750 was the first to use a twin-beam aluminium frame – earlier models used cradle-type aluminium frames.

Twin SRAD (Suzuki Ram Air Direct) ducts flank the headlights. These feed cool, high-density air to the sealed airbox under the tank, boosting power at speed.

The rear tyre is a very wide 190-section radial. Later models returned to a narrower 180-section tyre, for quicker steering.

With a history dating back to 1985, Suzuki's GSX-R750 is one of the longest-running sports bikes in production. And although various updates over the years have transformed it, the GSX-R750 retains the essential race-replica character of the original design: a powerful, revvy 750cc (46ci) engine mounted in a lightweight, track-ready chassis.

There have been three major design updates over the years (and at least seven minor revamps). The first big change was

Under the bodywork, the GSX-R750 is pure sports bike, with all the mass centred on the compact engine unit, a massively stiff aluminium frame and a small, stubby subframe to hold the seat unit.

from an oil-cooled engine to a water-cooled motor in 1992. Then, in 1996, the trademark aluminium cradle frame was swapped for a twin-beam framed chassis. Finally, 1997 saw the adoption of fuel injection in the 'W' version shown here. In between these major revisions, there have been countless detail changes to the GSX-R750.

EXCELLENCE ON TRACK

This 'SRAD' version, first shown in late 1997, produced 101kw (135bhp) and weighed 179kg (394lb). It also debuted a number of advanced technologies, including the fuel injection system, which were to spread to the other bikes in Suzuki's range. The chassis looks conventional, but clever frame design makes it extremely light and stiff, and the ancillary chassis components are top-quality track-ready parts. The front brakes use Tokico six-piston calipers and 320mm (12.2in) discs, while the fully adjustable suspension is by Japanese firm Kayaba.

The GSX-R is a fine road bike, but it excels on track. Road use highlights the rather uncomfortable riding position, lack of pillion space and sharp throttle action and quick steering. But for circuit riding, the huge ground clearance, strong brakes, sharp steering and strong top-end power delivery all shine, confirming the GSX-R as one of the finest pure sports bikes ever produced.

Suzuki GSX-R750

Top speed:	233km/h (165mph)
Engine type:	749cc (46ci), l/c inline-four, 16-valve, DOHC
Max power:	101kw (135bhp) @ 12,500rpm
Frame type:	aluminium twin spar
Tyre sizes:	front 120/70 17, rear 190/50 17
Final drive:	chain
Gearbox:	six-speed
Weight:	179kg (394lb)

JAPAN

Suzuki GT750

Despite its large capacity and advanced design, Suzuki's powerful GT750 was more of a grand tourer than a pure sports bike, excess weight handicapping it against the competition.

This four-leading-shoe front drum brake marks the GT750 shown here as an early 1972 model. From 1973, the front brake was changed to more powerful twin discs with single-piston calipers.

Unusually for a two-stroke engine, the GT750 used 32mm (1.25in) CV-type carburettors.

The GT750 had a reliable electric starter motor, as well as a kickstart.

The GT750 frame used the frame technology of the time: a steel-tube double-cradle design. It was heavy and not really stiff enough for good handling.

The instruments include an engine temperature gauge and an electronic gear indicator display, as well as speedo, tacho and indicator lights.

Chrome crashbars protect the delicate water radiator. Cooling was so effective that the radiator's small electric fan was seldom needed.

The twin rear shocks are preload adjustable only.

The chromed exhaust system has four silencers for the engine's three cylinders. The two small lower silencers are linked to the centre cylinder.

JAPAN

By the late 1970s, most large-capacity Japanese bikes were inline-four, four-stroke designs. However, several manufacturers had dabbled with alternative powerplants before the four-strokes took over. Suzuki was no exception, trying out rotary Wankel engines and turbocharged designs, as well as big-bore two-strokes. Two-stroke designs such as the GT500 offered good performance for the period, despite using rather low-tech, air-cooled technology.

But in 1972 the firm released a new, high-tech design, the GT750. This three-cylinder design was novel in that it used water-

This stripdown shot reveals the two-stroke oil tank under the side panel below the seat, and the water radiator cap, normally hidden by a flap in front of the fuel tank.

cooling, a first for mainstream Japanese machinery. This advanced cooling system allowed much better control of the engine's internal clearances, at the expense of extra weight and complexity.

DISAPPOINTING PERFORMANCE

Once the GT750 was launched, it became clear that it was not a pure performance design, in the mould of Kawasaki's H2 air-cooled 750 triple. Rather, the GT750 was a grand touring machine, with comfortable accommodation, plush suspension and extensive equipment. A combination of the water-cooling equipment - radiator, hoses and pump - and heavyweight chassis components meant the GT was extremely heavy, at over 230kg (507lb). This excessive mass, combined with marginal drum brakes, poor ground clearance, mediocre tyres and soft suspension, consigned the GT750 to a touring role, rather than the performance superbike enthusiasts had hoped for.

Over the next six years, the GT750 was progressively improved, with a disc front brake, revised frame design and more power. By the time it was discontinued in 1978, emissions regulations, increasing fuel prices and improved four-stroke designs were sounding the death knell for large two-stroke motorcycles, so Suzuki now concentrated on its GS range of four-stroke machines.

Suzuki GT750

Top speed:	193km/h (120mph)
Engine type:	738cc (45ci), l/c inline-triple, two-stroke
Max power:	50kw (67bhp) @ 6500rpm
Frame type:	steel-tube double cradle
Tyre sizes:	front 3.25 x 19, rear 4.00 x 18
Final drive:	chain
Gearbox:	five-speed
Weight:	230kg (507lb)

Suzuki TL1000R

Launched the year after the TL1000S, Suzuki's TL1000R promised more committed track performance. But it never really lived up to this promise and had little racing success.

The differences between the TL1000R and S engines include lighter forged pistons, stronger conrods and higher lift camshafts. The fuel injection system also has two injectors per cylinder, rather than one.

Suzuki stuck with the rotary damper rear suspension setup used on the TL1000S, which uses a separate spring and rotary damper unit, rather than a conventional combined unit.

The front brakes were improved over the TL1000S, dual six-piston Tokico calipers biting on floating 320mm (12.5in) discs.

The TL's maintenance-free battery is located behind a small flap on the left-hand fairing panels.

The aluminium rear swingarm has extensive stiffening braces underneath.

The rather outlandish 'duck-tail' seat cover can be replaced by a small pillion seat to carry a passenger.

The wide dual-beam headlight provides strong illumination.

The ram-airbox intakes are located in the high-pressure region at the front of the fairing, for best performance at speed.

The stainless-steel and aluminium two-into-two exhaust system features extremely high-set, tucked-in silencers.

Unveiled a year after the TL1000S, the TL1000R was a more track-oriented machine, which seemed to be aimed as much at superbike racing as road use. Like Honda, Suzuki's 750cc (46ci) four-cylinder GSX-R had failed to beat the Ducatis in World Superbike, and the TLR seemed like an attempt to benefit from the weight and capacity advantages of a 1000cc (61ci) twin.

The TL1000R used a revised version of the 'S' engine, with different valve timing and fuel injection settings to produce more top-end power. The engine was fitted to a

The stripped-down TL1000R reveals its twin-beam aluminium frame, large-volume sealed airbox and bolt-on rear subframe. The frame race kit offers adjustable steering head and swingarm pivot points.

supersports chassis, with a stiff aluminium beam frame, upside-down front forks and six-piston front brake calipers.

The TL1000R's appearance was striking: a full race fairing swept down over the front wheel, and the radical 'duck tail' pillion seat cover enhanced aerodynamic performance.

LIMITED SUCCESS

Unfortunately, when the TLR appeared on the streets, it failed to live up to its impressive appearance. Although lighter and shorter than Ducati's 916, at 190kg (419lb) with a 1405mm (55.3in) wheelbase, the TLR had much less refined handling and felt heavier and longer. The handling problems of the TL1000S led Suzuki to fit a steering damper as standard to the TLR, and this cheap, unadjustable damper unit further eroded the TLR's steering finesse.

The engine was universally praised, though, its strong top end providing a thrilling ride, while remaining flexible and torquey in the midrange. Indeed, the engine earned WSB honours - just not in a Suzuki. Bimota's TL1000-engined SB8R won a wet Australian superbike race in 2000, ridden by Anthony Gobert.

The TL1000R won limited success, on track and in showrooms. Suzuki's four-cylinder GSX-R range offered superior performance, and the TL range was discontinued in 2002.

Suzuki TL1000R

Top speed:	270km/h (168mph)
Engine type:	996cc (61ci), l/c 90° V-twin, eight-valve, DOHC
Max power:	101kw (135bhp) @ 9500rpm
Frame type:	aluminium twin spar
Tyre sizes:	front 120/70 17, rear 190/50 17
Final drive:	chain
Gearbox:	six-speed
Weight:	190kg (419lb)

JAPAN

Suzuki TL1000S

The TL1000S was Suzuki's first attempt at a V-twin sports bike, but a flawed chassis meant it never achieved the heights of the firm's four-cylinder machines.

Four-piston front brakes work well, but many owners upgraded their bikes with stronger six-piston calipers from the TL1000R or GSX-R750.

The TL1000S was recalled following complaints about instability, and a small steering damper was fitted transversely in front of the fuel tank.

The Mikuni/Denso fuel injection uses large 52mm (2in) throttle bodies.

The TL engine was an advanced design for 1997. The cylinder bores were coated with a ceramic material, the valvetrain used a combined chain/gear drive to save space and the engine case covers are lightweight magnesium and plastic.

The TL's clutch has a back-torque limiter to prevent the high-compression engine locking the rear wheel when the throttle is closed in lower gears.

The twin black intake tubes lead to a sealed ram-airbox. The cool, high-pressure air from these ducts boosts power at high speeds.

The two-into-two exhaust system is stainless steel and aluminium. The silencers are high-mounted to improve cornering ground clearance.

It has long been said, perhaps unfairly, that Japanese firms have built success on taking what other companies have built, then improving it. Suzuki's TL1000S is an indicator that this is not always the case.

Like most observers, Suzuki watched the success of Ducati's 916 superbike throughout the early 1990s. And in 1997, it launched a V-twin sports bike to compete with the Italian superbike, the TL1000S.

On paper, there looked to be no contest between the two bikes. The TLS had more power than the 916 (93kw/125bhp against 81kw/109bhp) and considerably less weight

The stripdown picture shows the aluminium trellis frame layout, large airbox and bolt-on rear subframe. The rear suspension spring is also visible behind the frame rail, separate from the rotary damper unit.

(187kg/412lb versus 203kg/447lb). It had more radical chassis technology, in the shape of a unique rotary-type rear damper unit with separate coil spring, and a trellis-type aluminium frame. The front end was also impressive, with fully adjustable upside-down forks.

FACTORY RECALL

While the TL's fuel-injected, eight-valve water-cooled engine was impressive, however, with excellent low and midrange power, the chassis was less notable. The rear damper had trouble dealing with hard sports riding, as did the unimpressive standard tyres, and some riders complained of instability from the steering, especially under hard acceleration.

A factory recall followed, to fit a steering damper, and there were other minor recalls to repair some engine reliability problems. Honda's Firestorm, launched at the same time, was a less controversial bike and did better in the showroom and on the forecourt. The bad publicity surrounding the TL's wayward handling and factory recalls affected sales, but the reputation (and associated low showroom prices) soon attracted many riders looking for a cheap, exciting machine. Nevertheless, the TL1000S was never a big success for Suzuki, and the model was discontinued in 2002.

Suzuki TL1000S

Top speed:	257km/h (160mph)
Engine type:	996cc (61ci), l/c 90° V-twin, eight-valve, DOHC
Max power:	93kw (125bhp) @ 9000rpm
Frame type:	aluminium trellis
Tyre sizes:	front 120/70 17, rear 190/50 17
Final drive:	chain
Gearbox:	six-speed
Weight:	187kg (412lb)

JAPAN

Suzuki GSF1200 Bandit

Launched a year after the successful Bandit 600, the Bandit 1200 brought the same great value, good performance and attractive style to the big-bore roadster class.

The attractive, sculpted steel fuel tank holds 19l (4.2 gal) of unleaded petrol, enough for 320km (200 miles) of gentle touring or 240km (150 miles) if ridden harder.

Twin grabrails, low-set footpegs and a broad, well-padded seat makes the Bandit a comfy ride for passengers.

The Bandit's front forks are conventional 43mm (1.7in) parts, adjustable for spring preload only.

The Bandit's torquey engine characteristics mean a five-speed gearbox is sufficient for rapid progress. Clutch actuation is hydraulic.

The rear suspension uses an aluminium swingarm operating a monoshock unit adjustable for spring preload and rebound damping.

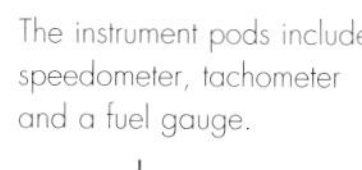

The instrument pods include speedometer, tachometer and a fuel gauge.

From the front, the Bandit's large chrome headlight, twin horns, chromed instrument pods and mirrors give it a classic, handsome style.

The four-into-one exhaust system is a high-quality stainless-steel and aluminium construction, but it is rather restrictive. Aftermarket race silencers can release as much as 12kw (15bhp) extra peak power.

It is not uncommon for the success of a smaller model to encourage a motorcycle firm to produce a larger version. The risks of development are, of course, less with a middleweight machine, and a 'big-bore' version stands a good chance of attracting maturing owners of the smaller machine.

So as Suzuki's GSF600 Bandit became a success, the release of a bigger Bandit seemed inevitable. The 1200 Bandit appeared a year after the 600, and it was just

Stripped down, the Bandit's simple design is obvious: big engine in a colour-matched steel-tube frame, with suspension and wheels at both ends. The small airbox fits below the seat area.

as big a hit. The recipe for the 1200 model was the same: take an old, mature engine design, fit it to a tried and tested chassis package, add a dash of retro styling and sell at a competitive price.

This time, however, the engine was a much more potent package - a big-bore 1157cc (71ci) version of the GSX-R1100K engine, retuned with softer camshafts and smaller carburettors. The result was a peak power figure of about 75kw (100bhp), with muscular power delivery.

FAIRING AND HALF-FAIRING

Following the 600's lead, the 1200 Bandit used a simple steel-tube cradle-type frame. Four-piston front brake calipers were by Tokico, and worked well, with above average power and feel for a budget bike.

Unlike with the 600 Bandit, Suzuki did not wait before launching a faired version of the 1200, and a half-faired Bandit 1200 was available immediately. This faired bike made a sound tourer for riders who were on a budget and was more comfortable at motorway speeds.

The 1200 Bandit was updated in 2001 with better six-piston front brake calipers, a new frame and engine revisions. The faired bike also featured a new, more aerodynamic screen, projector-type headlights and a new instrument panel.

Suzuki GSF1200 Bandit

Top speed:	225km/h (140mph)
Engine type:	1157cc (71ci), a/c inline-four, 16-valve, DOHC
Max power:	75kw (100bhp) @ 8500rpm
Frame type:	steel-tube double cradle
Tyre sizes:	front 120/70 17, rear 180/55 17
Final drive:	chain
Gearbox:	five-speed
Weight:	214kg (472lb)

JAPAN

Suzuki GSX1300R Hayabusa

Named after a Japanese falcon, Suzuki's Hayabusa knocked Honda's Super Blackbird off its perch by combining a record-breaking top speed with great sportsbike handling.

A fully featured electronic dashboard includes a clock and fuel gauge.

The steel fuel tank holds 22l (4.8 gal), enough for a 320km (200-mile) fuel range.

This aerodynamic tail hump can be replaced by a pillion seat and bolt-on grabrail for carrying a passenger.

The Hayabusa engine is a compact design, with advanced features, including a balancer shaft to reduce vibration and ceramic-plated cylinders.

The rear aluminium swingarm is massively braced by a large structural box and twin triangulated struts.

Features such as the enveloping front mudguard, narrow 'stacked' dual headlight and bulbous fairing are all designed to ensure minimal drag at high speeds.

A four-into-two exhaust system is used to improve mid-range torque.

Japanese tyre company Bridgestone produced a special version of its sticky BT56 sports tyre, designed to handle the extreme speeds and power of the GSX1300R.

The current high point for unlimited hypersports-class machines, Suzuki's GSX1300R Hayabusa is a massively powerful, hugely fast machine. It is capable of almost 322km/h (200mph), thanks to its 130kw (175bhp) engine and extremely efficient aerodynamic performance.

Launched in 1999, the Hayabusa was aimed at high-powered machines such as Honda's CBR1100XX Super Blackbird and Kawasaki's ZZ-R1100. Like these bikes, the Hayabusa (which takes its name from a Japanese falcon) offered spacious accommodation, a very high top speed and a strong, large-capacity engine. But unlike these competitors, the Hayabusa managed to combine this with a distinctly sporty nature. Although rather heavy for a sports

The twin air intakes either side of the headlight, seen here, are specially shaped to increase the volume of air into the engine. Even the indicators on the outside fairing are curved, to channel more air at high speeds.

bike at 215kg (474lb) dry, the GSX1300R's chassis delivers super handling, even during track use. Its 43mm (1.7in) upside-down front forks and rear monoshock are fully adjustable, and dual Tokico six-piston front brake calipers provide impressive stopping power. A small steering damper mounted behind the headlight enhances the Hayabusa's stability under acceleration, and a fully featured dashboard includes the full range of instruments, including a 355km/h (220mph) speedometer.

ESTABLISHED PRINCIPLES

The Hayabusa's engineering is impressive, but not exceptional - the chassis is built around a typical Japanese aluminium frame, with standard sportsbike suspension and brake components. The engine uses design principles first developed on the firm's GSX-R750, but is a conventional 16-valve water-cooled design, with double overhead cams and a single balance shaft running off the crankshaft. Carburation is by fuel injection, the 46mm (1.8in) throttle bodies being fed by an advanced ram-air pressurized airbox, which takes air from the scoops next to the headlight. At speed, these scoops collect high-pressure air, increasing engine power.

Oddly, earlier Hayabusas go faster than later bikes: Suzuki fitted the Hayabusa with a 300km/h (186mph) speed limiter in 2001.

Suzuki GSX1300R Hayabusa

Top speed:	300km/h (186mph)
Engine type:	1298cc (79ci), l/c inline-four, 16-valve, DOHC
Max power:	130kw (175bhp) @ 9800rpm
Frame type:	aluminium twin spar
Tyre sizes:	front 120/70 17, rear 190/50 17
Final drive:	chain
Gearbox:	six-speed
Weight:	215kg (474lb)

Triumph TT600

Triumph's first 600cc supersports bike, the TT600, was not a complete success. It offered great handling, but questionable engine performance and bland styling let it down.

43mm (1.7in) front forks are fully adjustable for spring preload, rebound and compression damping. Dual rate springs give a compliant ride.

Fuel capacity is 18l (3.96 gal).

Pillion accommodation is reasonable, although there is no grabrail as standard. Aftermarket rails improve matters for a passenger.

The TT600's engine is a conventional design, with four cylinders, rather than Triumph's trademark three-cylinder layout.

High-set footpegs, a narrow chassis and careful exhaust design all help the TT attain excellent ground clearance.

Though less protective than some other 600s, the TT's full fairing and windscreen do keep the worst of the wind and weather off the rider.

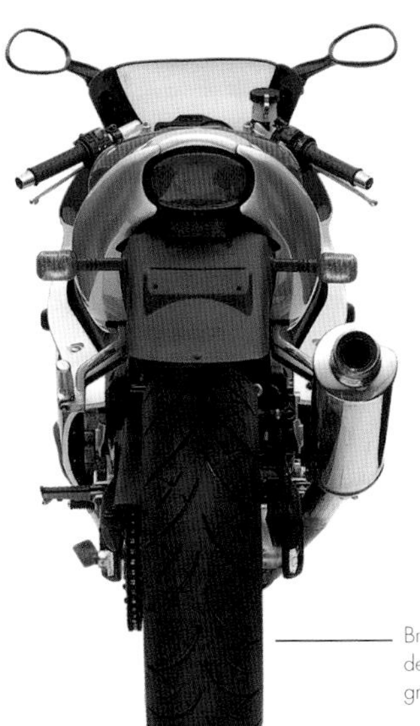

From the front, the TT's rounded headlight and bulbous fairing give it a rather dated look, compared with the Japanese competition.

Bridgestone BT-010 tyres helped the TT deliver stable handling and offered great grip. The rear tyre is a wide 180/55 17.

By 2000, the modern Triumph firm had fitted itself into a comfortable niche, producing well-built, stylish motorcycles, but without directly competing with mainstream Japanese products. All that was to change with the launch of the TT600. The supersports 600cc (37ci) class is perhaps the most closely contested in motorcycling, and it was an incredibly brave move for Triumph to enter this tough market.

When it appeared, the TT's statistics were encouraging: a dry weight of 170kg (374lb) and a 80kw (108bhp) power output put it in the same performance ballpark as

The basis of the TT's great handling is its stiff, lightweight aluminium beam frame, revealed in this stripdown shot. The black ram-air intake tubes can also be seen below the handlebars, leading through the frame rails.

Honda's CBR600. The TT was also well equipped, with electronic fuel injection and high-specification chassis components.

But when the TT600 hit the streets, it did not entirely live up to expectations, and the machine felt like it had not been fully developed. The fuel injection system, by French firm Sagem, was poorly developed and gave poor running at low engine speeds. Peak engine output was less than the competition, and the revvy nature of the power meant it was hard work to get the best from the TT.

PURE DYNAMISM

What did impress was the chassis. The TT's aluminium beam frame, fully adjustable suspension and brakes worked together superbly, giving a dynamic, high-quality ride. The little Triumph steered beautifully, was stable in all circumstances and had excellent cornering ground clearance. In addition, the TT's four-piston caliper brakes were among the best on any bike, with incredible power and subtle feel.

The feeling that the TT600 had been rushed out before it was completely ready was reinforced by a series of engine updates. New fuelling maps and altered internals gradually improved power delivery, although the TT still lacked the crispness of a well-injected machine such as Suzuki's GSX-R600.

Triumph TT600

Top speed:	248km/h (155mph)
Engine type:	599cc (37ci), l/c inline-four, 16-valve, DOHC
Max power:	80kw (108bhp) @ 12,750rpm
Frame type:	aluminium twin spar
Tyre sizes:	front 120/70 17, rear 180/55 17
Final drive:	chain
Gearbox:	six-speed
Weight:	170kg (374lb)

Triumph Thunderbird Sport

Taking styling and inspiration from Triumph's sporting past, the Thunderbird Sport is a refreshingly alternative way to celebrate the machines of yesteryear, with modern convenience and performance.

Hand-painted coachlines finish off the shapely 15l (3.3 gal) fuel tank perfectly.

Dual front-brake calipers are sliding twin-piston types, with braided steel hydraulic lines. They are powerful, but lack the feel of Triumph's sportsbike brakes.

Using a spine-type frame compelled Triumph to fit the air cleaner box behind the engine, compromising its capacity and the design of the carburettor intakes.

Despite its otherwise classic retro design, the Sport uses a modern adjustable monoshock rear suspension, with aluminium box-section swingarm, rather than a traditional twin shock layout.

The rear end is totally traditional, with chromed bullet indicators, large mudguard and a huge chrome and red tail light.

The adjustable sports front forks have triple-rate internal springs, to give a compliant yet firm ride.

The beautiful three-into-two stainless-steel exhaust system has twin silencers mounted on the right-hand side. Later models had one silencer on each side.

Much of Triumph's modern success has been down to the way the firm managed to combine its considerable motorcycling heritage with modern design and performance. The Thunderbird Sport is an example of this policy, combining as it does traditional 'retro' styling with a dashing, sporty edge.

The starting point for the Thunderbird Sport is the basic Thunderbird roadster, which uses the 885cc (54ci) Triumph triple engine in a steel-tube spine frame. However, the chassis components and the styling have been heavily overhauled, echoing the custom dirt-track styling of 1970s Triumph racers in the USA.

Removing the fuel tank, seat and side panels shows the large-diameter steel-tube backbone frame, from which the engine is hung. It is a stiff design, but compromises weight and raises the centre of gravity.

The standard, unadjustable suspension from the Thunderbird is replaced by fully adjustable, sporting front forks and rear monoshock. Twin front brake discs offer much better stopping power than the Thunderbird's single disc, while wider 43cm (17in) wire-spoked wheels wear sticky, sporting tyres.

IMPRESSIVE STYLING

Dominating the Sport's styling is a pair of upswept chrome silencers mounted on the right-hand side. Together with a fake chrome, 'pancake', air-filter housing and the dashing two-tone paint scheme, the exhausts make for a very stylish cosmetic package. Triumph's renowned build quality also imparts a classy feel to the bike.

The uprated parts also make a difference to the engine's performance: the Hinckley triple engine produces 61kw (82bhp), an increase of 10kw (13bhp) over the standard Thunderbird's 51kw (69bhp).

On the road, the Sport is a very pleasant machine to ride, the uprated chassis helping to make the most of the engine's tractable power delivery. There is ample ground clearance for committed cornering, and the suspension gives plush, controlled damping.

Only the front brakes let the bike down, the dual twin-piston calipers and 310mm (12.2in) discs giving lacklustre performance.

Triumph Thunderbird Sport

Top speed:	209km/h (130mph)
Engine type:	885cc (54ci), l/c inline-triple, 12-valve, DOHC
Max power:	61kw (82bhp) @ 8000rpm
Frame type:	steel-tube spine
Tyre sizes:	front 120/70 17, rear 160/60 17
Final drive:	chain
Gearbox:	six-speed
Weight:	224kg (493lb)

Triumph Daytona 955i

Triumph's premier sports bike has a soulful three-cylinder engine and a chassis designed to give superb performance on the road, rather than precise racetrack handling.

Cutouts in the aerodynamic fairing allow hot air to escape from the radiators and engine.

Although the 955i has a passenger seat, it is cramped and uncomfortable. A single-seat cover comes as standard, improving looks when riding solo.

The first 955i design, the T595 Daytona, had problems with the front exhaust pipes touching down during committed track riding, causing the bike to crash. The 955i corrected this with a more tucked-in stainless-steel exhaust system.

Modern Triumphs offer excellent build quality, and the 955i's components resist corrosion admirably, particularly aluminium parts such as footrests and levers.

Triumph fairing panels are made from tough, shatterproof plastic, which resists minor damage very well.

The 955i's conventional 45mm (1.8in) front forks are very strong and stiff, and are adjustable for spring preload, rebound and compression damping.

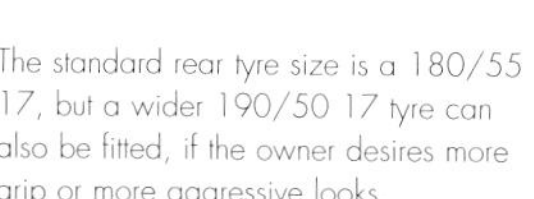

The standard rear tyre size is a 180/55 17, but a wider 190/50 17 tyre can also be fitted, if the owner desires more grip or more aggressive looks.

When Triumph re-emerged as a modern motorcycle builder in 1991, it began by building a modular range of machines, with shared components to save costs. While this policy produced a range of sound motorbikes, it did restrict the abilities of the firm to produce a cutting-edge sports bike to compete with bikes such as Honda's FireBlade.

But by 1996, Triumph's success allowed it to invest the money required to build such a bike. Released in 1997, the T595 Daytona,

Triumph's strong, reliable three-cylinder engine is used to strengthen the aluminium tube perimeter frame, improving handling. The forward-facing air intakes can be seen below the steering head.

as it was called, put Triumph firmly in contention as a serious sportsbike maker. It used a water-cooled, inline-triple engine, but this engine was a much more advanced design than the older modular triples. It was also fuel-injected, a first for the firm. The chassis was also filled with Triumph firsts: its first aluminium frame and an attractive single-sided swingarm. Public reaction was favourable, despite a serious of press reports about suspect build quality and a recall for the frame. The new Triumph managed to combine the character and styling of a European three-cylinder machine with the performance of the Japanese four-cylinder sports bikes. The only suspect area was its weight - the T595 was 18kg (40lb) heavier than the FireBlade at 198kg (436lb) dry.

STEADY IMPROVEMENT

In 1998, the T595 was renamed the 955i Daytona and received a few updates, which improved ground clearance, refined the suspension settings and enhanced the Sagem fuel injection. But it was in 2001 that the Daytona took the next step forward in performance. A programme of weight loss and power increases produced a machine weighing 188kg (414lb) while producing 110kw (147bhp). The single-sided swingarm was replaced with a lighter double-sided part, and the bodywork was all-new.

Triumph Daytona 955i

Top speed:	272km/h (170mph)
Engine type:	955cc (58ci), l/c inline-triple, 12-valve, DOHC
Max power:	110kw (147bhp) @ 10,700rpm
Frame type:	aluminium tube perimeter
Tyre sizes:	front 120/70 17, rear 180/55 17
Final drive:	chain
Gearbox:	six-speed
Weight:	188kg (414lb)

TRIUMPH SPEED TRIPLE

With a high-horsepower three-cylinder engine, sportsbike-derived chassis components and bags of attitude, Triumph's Speed Triple is a streetfighting city bike par excellence.

Wide, flat handlebars give an upright riding position and provide direct steering control.

The Triple's plastic petrol tank holds 21l (4.6 gal) of unleaded petrol.

Like the rest of Triumph's 955 triple range, the multipoint sequential fuel injection system is made by French firm Sagem.

The Speed Triple proudly shows off its engine. The three-cylinder, in-line layout gives good balance, with its 120° crankshaft. Extensive development of the cylinder head gives strong peak power, with a good spread of torque.

A small instrument panel includes speedometer, tachometer and temp gauge. Later models feature a lighter display unit, with an LCD panel.

A small, neat oil-cooling radiator is mounted vertically in front of the engine.

The exhaust system is an all-stainless-steel three-into-one design. Triumph offers various racing silencers for aftermarket off-road use.

Cast aluminium three-spoke wheels are fitted with wide, sticky radial sports tyres.

Between its plastic-clad sports range and its chrome-plated retro range, Triumph launched a new, café-racer styled bike in 1994. Called the Speed Triple, the new bike offered all the sporting prowess of the firm's Daytona flagship sportster, in an aggressive naked design.

The first model was built around the firm's Daytona 900 triple, with an 885cc (54ci) carburetted engine, steel spine frame and sporting chassis components.

Over the years, as Triumph updated its premier sports bike, the Speed Triple followed. So, by 1999, the Speed Triple had

The Speed Triple has minimal bodywork, so little more is revealed when it is stripped down. The airbox is mounted between the frame tubes, and the seat unit is supported by an aluminium subframe.

evolved into this 88kw (118bhp), 189kg (417lb) high-performance machine, which used essentially the same chassis and engine as the 955i Daytona.

Aggressive, brutal design had always been part of the Triple's allure, and this latest model is no different. The plastic fairing of the Daytona is swapped for a pair of chrome-plated headlights, with only a small instrument pod and maybe an optional flyscreen to deflect the windblast over the rider. The fuel-injected 12-valve 955cc (58ci) triple engine is retuned for even stronger midrange power delivery, at the expense of peak power output.

ALL-ROUND PERFORMER

The rest of the bike closely follows the Daytona design, with an aluminium tube perimeter frame, fully adjustable 45mm (1.8in) forks and a fully adjustable rear monoshock, together with Triumph's excellent front brakes.

The Speed Triple (the name echoes the Speed Twin Triumph from the 1950s) is at home with most types of riding, short of long-distance touring. The strong engine, upright riding position and superb brakes make it a fine city bike, perfect for splitting traffic queues and café posing. The track-developed chassis also gives great circuit performance, and the Triple is a superb back-road bike, too.

Triumph Speed Triple

Top speed:	240km/h (150mph)
Engine type:	955cc (58ci), l/c inline-triple, 12-valve, DOHC
Max power:	88kw (118bhp) @ 9100rpm
Frame type:	aluminium tube perimeter
Tyre sizes:	front 120/70 17, rear 190/50 17
Final drive:	chain
Gearbox:	six-speed
Weight:	189kg (416lb)

Triumph Sprint ST

Triumph's Sprint ST is a modern, high-performance sports-touring motorcycle, based on the firm's flagship 955i sports bike. It is one of Triumph's most capable designs.

Triumph's four-piston dual front-brake calipers, biting on 320mm (12.5in) floating discs, give good stopping power and feedback.

Although its plastic fuel tank holds just 19.5l (4.3 gal), the Sprint's modest fuel consumption allows a decent fuel range of around 320km (200 miles).

As befits a sports-touring bike, the Sprint has a large, comfortable dual seat, pillion grabrail and relaxing seating positions for rider and passenger.

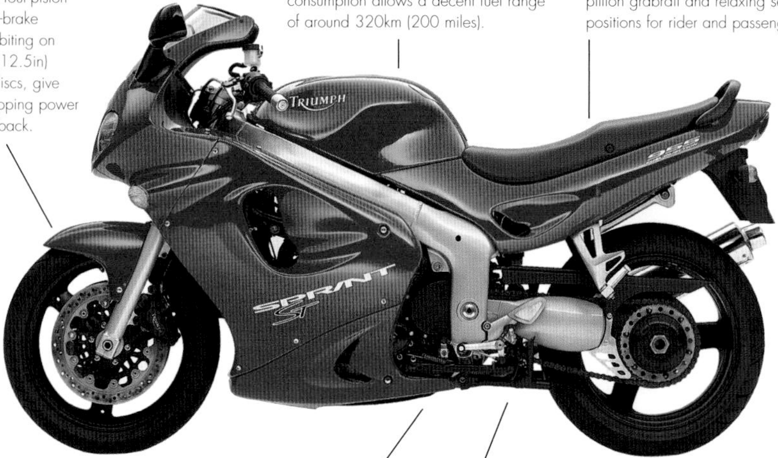

The Sprint ST is a very practical machine, with useful touring features such as a centre stand and low-set foot rests.

The single-sided swingarm comes from the 955i and is made from cast aluminium. Making rear wheel removal straightforward, it also helps with wheel maintenance.

The twin headlights and wide-set rearview mirrors help the Sprint rider see clearly both ahead and behind, by day and night.

The large-capacity stainless-steel silencer can be moved downwards to allow hard luggage panniers to be fitted.

Triumph is open about its policy for developing new motorcycles. It identifies market leaders, analyses their performance parameters and aims at least to match these with a new model.

In the case of the T595 Daytona sports bike, the market leader analysed was Honda's FireBlade, while in the case of the Sprint ST, the target machine was the Honda VFR800. The VFR 750 and 800 were the definitive sports tourers throughout the 1990s, and Triumph targeted the best to produce the Sprint ST, which was launched in late 1998.

With its protective full fairing removed, the Sprint looks just like a sports bike, with its stiff aluminium beam frame, bolt-on rear subframe and large airbox.

The Sprint was built around a version of the 955cc (58ci) triple engine first used in the T595. This advanced, fuel-injected engine was retuned for more midrange power, then installed in a classic sports-tourer chassis. A stiff, sporty aluminium frame wore sports-grade suspension front and rear, with an attractive single-sided rear swingarm and aerodynamic bodywork. However, this sporting design was married to a more practical outlook: the riding position was slightly more upright, the dual seat has considerable pillion space and the windscreen offers good wind protection.

POWER AND RELIABILITY

The Sprint's performance figures closely mirrored the then-current VFR, and indeed the Triumph was lighter and more powerful by 1kg (2.2lb) and 0.75kw (1bhp), respectively. Riding the Sprint was also a very satisfying experience: the Triumph enjoyed fine handling, with the trademark Triumph brakes in particular standing out. The triple engine combined a soulful sound and strong power delivery with smooth, economical running and fine reliability.

The Sprint ST had a mild update in 2002, when it received an even more powerful 955 engine. This was based on the latest Daytona sportsbike engine, and peak power increased to almost 89kw (120bhp).

Triumph Sprint ST

Top speed:	256km/h (160mph)
Engine type:	955cc (58ci), l/c inline-triple, 12-valve, DOHC
Max power:	88kw (118bhp) @ 9100rpm
Frame type:	aluminium twin spar
Tyre sizes:	front 120/70 17, rear 180/55 17
Final drive:	chain
Gearbox:	six-speed
Weight:	207kg (456lb)

UNITED KINGDOM

TRIUMPH TROPHY 1200

Triumph's entry in the heavyweight touring market, the Trophy 1200 has a tempting mix of comfort and performance for two-up long-distance riding.

Triumph offers heated grips, anti-theft alarm and other touring conveniences as optional factory accessories.

A massive fuel tank holds 25l (5.5 gal), easily allowing a 320km (200-mile) fuel range at touring speeds.

The Trophy's colour-matched 32l (7 gal) capacity hard panniers became standard fitment in 1996. Triumph offers a rear luggage rack, topbox with backrest, and pannier inner bags as extra-cost parts.

A torquey, powerful design, the inline-four motor uses four 36mm (1.4in) Keihin carburettors, 16 valves and twin cams. A 900 version of the Trophy has a three-cylinder version of this engine, using the same pistons, valves and conrods.

A strong, easy-to-use centre stand is essential on a touring machine, particularly a chain-driven model, to allow easy rear wheel and driveline maintenance. A side stand is also fitted.

Large dual headlights provide powerful illumination of the road ahead at night. Chrome surround plate appeared in 1998.

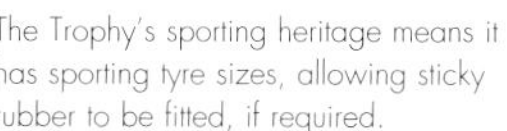

The Trophy's sporting heritage means it has sporting tyre sizes, allowing sticky rubber to be fitted, if required.

One of the first of the new-generation 'Hinckley' Triumphs launched in 1991, the Trophy 1200 is a powerful, heavyweight sports tourer. Built around Triumph's modular design, the Trophy uses a 1180cc (72ci) inline-four cylinder engine fitted into the spine-type frame common to all the first-generation Triumphs. Like all early modern Triumphs, the spine frame means the Trophy is much heavier than more modern designs, and it carries its weight high, making it rather awkward at low speeds.

The first Trophy was less obviously a touring machine than later designs. The bodywork was not so protective, although

The Trophy's large-diameter steel-tube spine frame can be seen arching back over the engine.

it fitted well into the sport-touring market of the early 1990s. Against bikes such as Yamaha's FJ1200, the Trophy did well, Triumph's strong identity and build quality lifting it above the Japanese competition.

But as more sporting designs entered the sport-touring market, the Trophy slipped into a pure touring role. It was too heavy and underpowered, and the chassis components too limited to keep up with the competition.

REFINED STYLING

With this in mind, Triumph redesigned the Trophy in 1995, with a more touring-oriented layout. Bodywork was restyled, while new clocks and headlights improved touring convenience. Further design refinements over the years saw new stainless-steel exhausts, adjustable rear suspension and another fairing makeover.

By 1999, the Trophy had become a mature, accomplished design. The engine remained reliable, smooth and strong, while the bodywork was stylish and protective. The chassis was unsophisticated compared with Honda's Pan European, but still eminently capable, with strong brakes and compliant suspension. Indeed, as a long-distance tourer, the only remaining black mark against the Trophy was its lack of shaft final drive: an update long demanded by serious touring Triumph fans.

Triumph Trophy 1200

Top speed:	224km/h (140mph)
Engine type:	1180cc (72ci), l/c inline-four, 16-valve, DOHC
Max power:	80kw (107bhp) @ 9000rpm
Frame type:	steel-tube spine
Tyre sizes:	front 120/70 17, rear 170/60 17
Final drive:	chain
Gearbox:	six-speed
Weight:	235kg (518lb)

YAMAHA FZS600 FAZER

One of the most practical budget roadsters available, Yamaha's Fazer still comes with a healthy dose of excitement, and thrilling performance.

An all-round machine such as the Fazer has to provide a decent level of pillion accommodation. The spacious dual seat and low-set pegs are very comfortable, even over the 290km (180-mile) plus fuel range of the Fazer.

The Fazer's four-piston front calipers are high-specification parts, shared with the firm's cutting-edge R-series sports machines. They bite on 298mm (11.7in) floating discs for excellent stopping performance.

Compared to the Thundercat engine, the Fazer has small 33mm (1.2in) carburettors, to improve midrange power. The engine cylinders are more upright, with cosmetic finning.

A small half-fairing holds twin square headlights (later updated to a twin fox-eye design) and a traditional dashboard with analogue speedometer and tachometer.

This model of the Fazer has a painted steel four-into-one exhaust system, with a stainless silencer. Later models had a full stainless-steel exhaust.

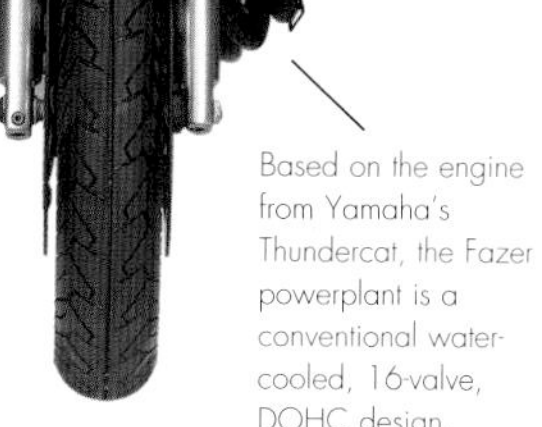

Based on the engine from Yamaha's Thundercat, the Fazer powerplant is a conventional water-cooled, 16-valve, DOHC design.

The middleweight all-rounder class is one which became increasingly important for manufacturers in the mid-1990s. Bikes such as Suzuki's GSX600 Bandit had proved that there was a strong market for affordable, fun machines which had an element of performance, stylish design and practicality.

When it launched in 1997, Yamaha's Fazer 600 managed to excel in all these areas – its Thundercat-derived engine was strong, flexible and economical, a steel-tube frame gave impressive handling and the half-fairing made it a sound long-distance performer. Clever component choice, especially in the R1-sourced front brakes, allowed what was

Yamaha engineers chose a cheap (if heavy) double-cradle steel-tube frame and aluminium box-section swingarm for the Fazer 600. This setup gives excellent stiffness and has a good price/ performance ratio.

almost sportsbike performance, as well as sensible real-world usefulness.

The Fazer's engine was slightly altered from the Thundercat design. Smaller carburettors increased midrange torque, and the cylinders were set more upright to fit the steel-tube frame.

MATCHING THE COMPETITION

On the road, the Fazer 600 is an impressive performer. The engine is strong in the midrange and has been described as the perfect roadbike engine. The front brakes are incredibly strong and more than capable of overwhelming the soft front suspension, while the budget rear monoshock is rather soft for hard sports riding. Perhaps the major handicap to its cornering performance, though, are the low-set footpegs and exhaust, which reduce ground clearance during track riding. Other criticisms of the first Fazer 600 centred on the poor head-lights and rust-prone exhaust system. But updates in both 2000 and 2002 addressed these issues, with a new top fairing and headlight design and stainless-steel exhaust, as well as increased fuel capacity,

These small convenience improvements kept the Fazer 600 at the top of the middleweight all-rounder tree, despite improvements to Honda's Hornet 600 and Suzuki's Bandit 600 and SV650.

Yamaha FZS600 Fazer

Top speed:	232km/h (145mph)
Engine type:	599cc (37ci), l/c inline-four, 16-valve, DOHC
Max power:	71kw (95bhp) @ 11,500rpm
Frame type:	steel-tube double cradle
Tyre sizes:	front 110/70 17, rear 160/60 17
Final drive:	chain
Gearbox:	six-speed
Weight:	188kg (414lb)

Yamaha YZF600R Thundercat

While less overtly sporty than its competitors, Yamaha's Thundercat offers great performance in an attractive, practical, everyday sports-touring package.

While the Thundercat's frame is heavy and unfashionable painted steel, rather than aluminium, it is still plenty stiff and light enough for most riders' needs.

The large dual seat has plenty of room for rider and pillion, and a pair of grab handles either side allow the passenger to hold on under acceleration and braking.

Developed from the FZR600R engine, the Thundercat's engine is an unremarkable, 16-valve inline-four design.

The Thundercat's monoshock rear swingarm is a light, stiff aluminium design.

The Thundercat has rather Spartan instruments, with no fuel gauge or clock. The 19l (4.2 gal) fuel tank uses a reserve warning light when the fuel level is low.

The black-finished four-into-one exhaust design is made of mild steel, which can suffer from corrosion when the paint wears off.

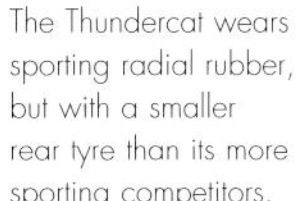

The Thundercat wears sporting radial rubber, but with a smaller rear tyre than its more sporting competitors.

Released at the same time as Yamaha's 1000cc (61ci) Thunderace, the Thundercat has followed a familiar path for successful sports bikes. Initially launched as a 600cc (37ci) supersport model, the Thundercat performed admirably, offering the usability of Honda's CBR600F, while packing a performance punch almost equal to Kawasaki's ZX-6R. That combination came clothed in a dynamic, stylish full fairing with a strong resemblance to the Thunderace. A large single headlight sat above an aggressive ram-air intake, and the colourways were bold and attractive.

A large single air intake below the headlight feeds cool, dense air to the engine. The air intake tubes can clearly be seen running through the frame to the large airbox above the engine.

But as time passed, the competition moved on, and Yamaha introduced the R6. Suddenly, the Thundercat was too heavy, underpowered and unfashionable for the flagship 600 class, so it moved smoothly into a middleweight sports-tourer role.

That shift suits the Thundercat fine. Its four-cylinder engine delivered a more usable power delivery than some of its competitors, and the larger size of the Thundercat allows more comfortable accommodation for rider and pillion.

SPORTING PROWESS

But the Thundercat still offers a potent sporting package. Its suspension, while soft as standard, is adjustable and can easily be set up for a more aggressive riding style. The Thundercat's powerful Sumitomo brakes were always the best in class and are still used on the R6.

Where the Thundercat lags behind a little is in minor details – the dashboard is outdated and short on function, while the styling has aged and looks less dashing than it once did.

However, the Thundercat is an all-round machine. It works well as a daily commuter tool and is still good for weekend trackday or sporty road use. And for occasional two-up touring, it is preferable to the smaller, more focused bikes that have replaced it.

Yamaha YZF600R Thundercat

Top speed:	257km/h (160mph)
Engine type:	599cc (37ci), l/c inline-four, 16-valve, DOHC
Max power:	75kw (100bhp) @ 11,500rpm
Frame type:	Deltabox steel twin spar
Tyre sizes:	front 120/60 17, rear 160/60 17
Final drive:	chain
Gearbox:	six-speed
Weight:	187kg (411lb)

Yamaha YZF-R6

Light, short and with an incredibly powerful, peaky 600cc (37ci) engine, Yamaha's exhilarating YZF-R6 encapsulates the best characteristics of 600 supersports machinery.

The aluminium tube rear subframe holds the seats, tail unit and electrical ancillaries. It is a removable bolt-on design to simplify crash repair and allows replacement with lighter parts for racing.

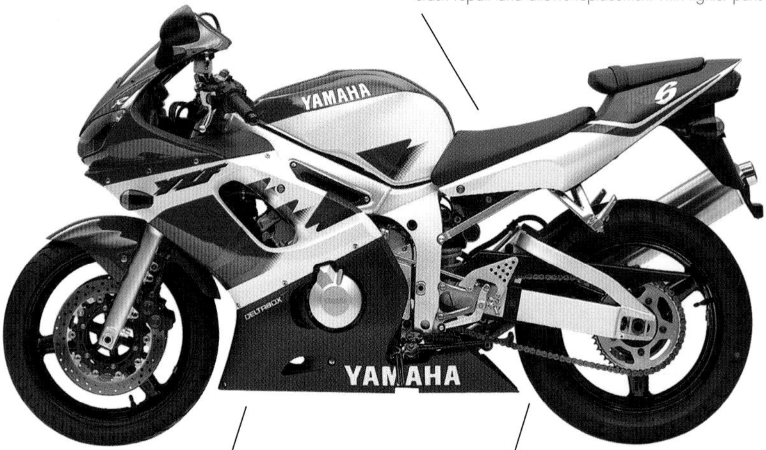

The R6's frame curves down towards the engine unit, which is used as a strengthening part of the chassis. This allows a lighter frame, without affecting stiffness.

The braced aluminium swingarm is both light and stiff.

The R6's most notable feature is a large air intake between the headlights, which is pressurized at speed with cool, dense air, further increasing peak power.

One easy way of quickly distinguishing the R6 from its larger capacity siblings is its right-way-up forks, rather than the upside-down parts of the R7 and R1.

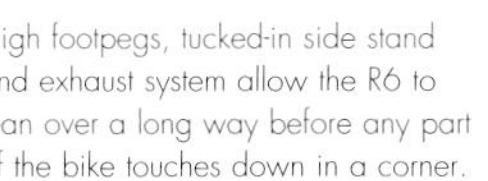
High footpegs, tucked-in side stand and exhaust system allow the R6 to lean over a long way before any part of the bike touches down in a corner.

Following the lead of its larger capacity sibling, the R1, which had been launched the year before, Yamaha's R6 brought the design excellence of the 'R' series to the competitive 600cc (37ci) class in late 1998. With 89kw (120bhp) claimed power and 169kg (373lb) claimed dry weight, the R6 was the lightest and most powerful in its category. Little, apart from the front brake calipers, was taken from its predecessor, the Thundercat, and the R6 used an all-new aluminium Deltabox

With bodywork removed, the engine's triangular layout can be seen from the side: the clutch sits behind and above the crankshaft end cover, while the gearbox output sprocket sits below the clutch shaft. This layout allows a much shorter, more compact engine.

frame with a high revving inline-four, 16-valve engine.

Although not dominating the class as the R1 had, the R6 impressed most riders with its compact chassis, strong, revvy engine and sharp, flighty handling. It was an exhilarating machine to ride, as befits a middleweight sports bike. That is due partly to the short wheelbase, but also down to the engine's power delivery: engine revs are best kept above 11,000rpm for best progress.

THOUGHTFUL DESIGN

Weight loss had been achieved by careful design in most components, particularly in the engine. Transmission was by wet clutch, six-speed gearbox and chain final drive.

The R6 also boasted fully adjustable suspension front and rear, which though soft as standard for track use, offers a good compromise for road riding. One aftermarket component many riders consider essential on the R6 is a good steering damper, the bike's sharp steering tending to instability under hard acceleration on bumpy roads.

By 2002, updated models from Honda, Kawasaki and Suzuki had pushed the R6 down the class rankings, so a heavily updated machine was released for 2003. This used advanced suction-piston type fuel injection and a new cast aluminium frame, improving handling and boosting power and drivability.

Yamaha YZF-R6

Top speed:	264km/h (164mph)
Engine type:	599cc (37ci), l/c inline-four, 16-valve, DOHC
Max power:	89kw (120bhp) @ 13,000rpm
Frame type:	aluminium twin spar
Tyre sizes:	front 120/60 17, rear 180/55 17
Final drive:	chain
Gearbox:	six-speed
Weight:	169kg (373lb)

JAPAN

Yamaha YZF-R7

Built for racers, Yamaha's YZF-R7 was sold to the public only to qualify it for World Superbike racing. Costing £21,500 ($32,000) when launched, it makes an exotic, rare sight on the road.

The R7 does not have large ram-air intake ducts, but many racers fit bolt-on intake ducts to increase power.

The black-finished aluminium frame has computer-designed bracing elements to increase stiffness without adding weight. The short, stubby rear subframe stops just below the riders seat: there is no passenger seat on the R7.

The Sumitomo four-piston brake calipers give excellent performance. But their mounting plates allow easy replacement by more exotic racing brake calipers.

The aluminium rear swingarm is extra-long to improve rear tyre traction and has extensive bracing either side for maximum stiffness.

The twin small 'fox-eye' projector-type headlights are uniquely shaped, instantly identifying the R7 from the front.

A lightweight, carbon-fibre silencer is mounted on a large-bore four-into-two-into-one exhaust system. An EXUP valve in the collector section alters exhaust characteristics, depending on engine speed, improving power delivery.

The 750cc (46ci) four-cylinder class has long been an important category in racing. So, although its importance waned in the early twenty-first century, many high-specification 'race-replica' machines were produced by Japanese companies.

The last and most advanced of these was Yamaha's R7. Launched in late 1999, the R7 completed Yamaha's 'R'-series super sport family – the R6 and R1 had been launched in 1998 and 1997, respectively. But while the R6 and R1 were mass-production bikes,

The R7 has a very advanced electronic fuel injection system, with two fuel injectors for each cylinder. In standard form, only one injector fires, but with Yamaha race parts, both injectors fire to give more power from the engine.

intended for general public sale, the R7 was an expensive, limited-edition race bike, aimed at professional racers.

The basic R7 layout is conventional, with a four-cylinder, water-cooled 749cc (46ci) engine in a twin-beam aluminium frame. The engine has Yamaha's trademark design motifs, including five valves per cylinder and a computer-controlled butterfly valve in the exhaust system. However, the engine has been designed for racing use, so both conrods and valves are made from tough, light titanium.

HIGH SPECIFICATION

What makes the R7 so special is the highly specified chassis. Both front forks, rear monoshock and steering damper are race-type parts made by Swedish suspension specialists Ohlins, and the Sumitomo brake calipers are the same used on the R1 and R6.

Despite its impressive specification, the R7 is not very powerful in standard trim. Yamaha produced only one version of the R7 for all world markets, so the standard bike generates just 75kw (100bhp) at the wheel, to comply with French and German power limits. However, by fitting Yamaha race-kit components, the power can be increased to more than 120kw (160bhp), making a derestricted R7 one of the most powerful sports bikes available.

Yamaha YZF-R7

Top speed:	265km/h (165mph)
Engine type:	749cc (46ci), l/c inline-four, 20-valve, DOHC
Max power:	79kw (106bhp) @ 11,000rpm
Frame type:	aluminium twin spar
Tyre sizes:	front 120/70 17, rear 180/55 17
Final drive:	chain
Gearbox:	six-speed
Weight:	176kg (388lb)

JAPAN

Yamaha YZF1000R Thunderace

Introduced to beat Honda's FireBlade, Yamaha's Thunderace turned out to be a stopgap between the venerable FZR1000R and its next-generation sports bike, the mighty R1.

A more extensive plastic fairing than on more modern designs allows the Thunderace rider much more protection from poor weather and windblast at speed.

The YZF1000's steel tank holds 20l (4.4 gal) of 95 octane unleaded petrol.

The broad, spacious dual seat is perfect for riding long distances, even with a passenger. There is no grabrail for the pillion, though, although many owners fit an aftermarket rail.

The engine has three inlet valves and two exhaust valves per cylinder – most bike engines have two inlet and two exhaust valves per cylinder. The resulting 20-valve layout is common on Yamaha sports bikes and helps provide strong engine power throughout the rev range.

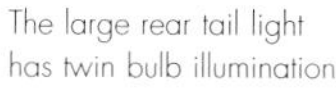

The large rear tail light has twin bulb illumination.

A wide, twin-beam headlight gives superb illumination of the road ahead at night.

The Thunderace is fitted with wide radial tyres, which give good grip and excellent stability.

When it was unveiled by Yamaha in 1996, the Thunderace was claimed to be a competitor to Honda's extremely successful FireBlade. With a claimed power output of 108kw (145bhp) and a chassis based upon the firm's YZF750 sports bike, the Thunderace looked close to the FireBlade on paper. But its excessive weight of 198kg (437lb) showed that the Thunderace was merely a stopgap for Yamaha, before the firm's YZF-R1 was released two years later.

In many ways, the Thunderace was a natural progression from the firm's previous flagship sports bike, the FZR1000 EXUP. The Thunderace engine is an updated

The EXUP valve is located in the exhaust system behind the fairing panel, below the engine. This variable valve gives excellent midrange power, while also allowing a strong top-end delivery.

version of the EXUP engine, with an inline-four, liquid-cooled, DOHC 20-valve layout. 'EXUP' refers to Yamaha's Exhaust Ultimate Powervalve system, which uses a computerized butterfly valve in the exhaust to alter its characteristics at different engine speeds.

EXCELLENT STABILITY

The YZF750-based chassis uses a stiff, light aluminium twin-beam frame, with 43mm (1.7in) conventional front forks and adjustable rear monoshock. The YZF1000R's Sumitomo front brake calipers became standard issue on Yamaha sports bikes. These were much better than the competition in 1996, and they continue to provide excellent performance in comparison to more modern designs.

On the road, the Thunderace's length and weight make it less manoeuvrable than smaller designs, particularly on twisty roads and race tracks. Conversely, these attributes make it extremely stable at the higher speeds made easy by the very strong engine. This stability at speed, together with reasonable handling and braking, has given the Thunderace a new lease of life as a fast sports tourer. While unable to compete with more modern litre-class sports bikes, its comfortable accommodation and strong performance makes it suitable for fast touring trips, even with a pillion aboard.

Yamaha YZF1000R Thunderace

Top speed:	274km/h (170mph)
Engine type:	1002cc (61ci), l/c inline-four, 20-valve, DOHC
Max power:	108kw (145bhp) @ 10,000rpm
Frame type:	aluminium twin spar
Tyre sizes:	front 120/70 17, rear 180/55 17
Final drive:	chain
Gearbox:	five-speed
Weight:	198kg (437lb)

JAPAN

Yamaha YZF-R1

With the dimensions and weight of a 600cc (37ci) sports bike, and the power of a full 1000cc (61ci) machine, Yamaha's YZF-R1 was a revelation when launched in 1997.

The year 2000 update saw a stiffer Deltabox frame and revised, more angular bodywork.

The R1's upside-down front forks have extra-long travel, to help keep the front wheel from touching the ground under hard acceleration.

The engine design includes a one-piece upper crankcase/cylinder unit, magnesium engine covers and lightweight internals, aimed at reducing engine mass.

A wide 190-section rear tyre is needed to provide sufficient grip for the R1's high power output.

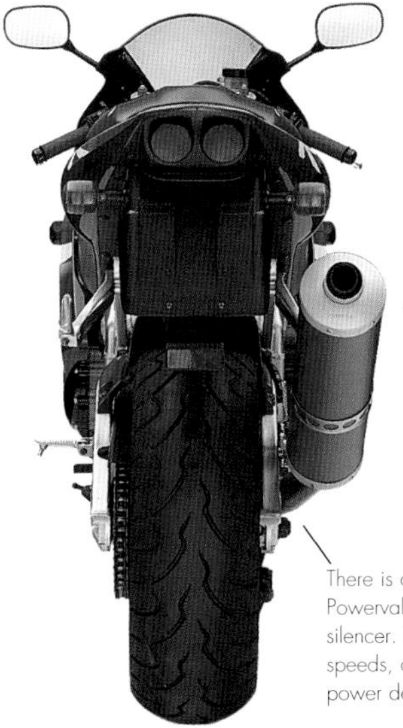

This blue-finished silencer is made from lightweight titanium and was introduced on the 2000 model update.

High-mounted footpegs and a narrow, tucked-in exhaust system give the R1 excellent ground clearance, allowing an incredible 56° lean angle.

There is a computer-controlled EXUP (EXhaust Ultimate Powervalve) valve in the exhaust system, upstream of the silencer. This valve moves position at different engine speeds, altering exhaust characteristics and improving power delivery at low to medium revs.

Every so often comes a machine which takes a leap forward in terms of performance for its class. Such was Honda's CBR900RR FireBlade in 1992, Ducati's 916 in 1993 - and Yamaha's R1 in 1997. Packing a 1l (0.2gal) punch though smaller and lighter than most 600-class machines, the R1 rewrote the 1000cc (61ci) sportsbike class rules, taking the crown worn by Honda's FireBlade since 1992.

The R1's designers achieved its remarkable performance by adopting a

Unlike competing models from Honda and Suzuki, Yamaha's R1 does not use a ram-air pressurized airbox with large external ducts to increase power at high speeds. Rather, it exploits a high-capacity, conventional design.

holistic approach to engine and chassis design. The layout of the engine was planned to improve chassis design, and great efforts were made to reduce mass and size in every part of the bike.

TOP OF THE CLASS

The engine was developed with a triangular architecture, in order to reduce length front-to-back. This layout placed the gearbox input shaft above the crankshaft and the gearbox output shaft, bringing the three shafts closer together and reducing engine length. The shorter, more compact engine was needed to optimize the chassis design. The aluminium swingarm could be longer, for increased rear wheel traction, while still allowing a short wheelbase. The Deltabox-type aluminium twin-beam frame combines great stiffness with light weight, and both the front forks and rear monoshock are fully adjustable, circuit-ready items. Four-piston brake calipers are similar to those used on the firm's Thunderace and provide excellent stopping power.

The R1's styling also put it straight to the top of its class. A sharp-nosed top fairing, twin fox-eye headlights and angular seat unit combined compact dimensions with aggressive lines. Updates in 2000 and 2002 further refined the R1 package with better handling and fuel injection.

Yamaha YZF-R1

Top speed:	290km/h (175mph)
Engine type:	998cc (61ci), l/c inline-four, 20-valve, DOHC
Max power:	113kw (152bhp) @ 10,500rpm
Frame type:	aluminium twin spar
Tyre sizes:	front 120/70 17, rear 190/50 17
Final drive:	chain
Gearbox:	six-speed
Weight:	174kg (384lb)

JAPAN

Yamaha VMX1200 V-Max

Unlike some custom-styled machines, Yamaha's V-Max really lives up to its brutal 'Hot-Rod' styling, offering incredible acceleration from its powerful V-four engine.

The 1993 model year update also saw larger diameter front forks fitted, up to 43mm (1.7in) from 40mm (1.6in).

The fuel tank is below the seat, accessed by a spring-loaded flap. The space above the engine where a fuel tank normally lives is taken up by the airbox, carburettors and electrics.

These four-piston brake calipers were introduced on the 1993 model year and offered much-improved stopping power over the original single-piston floating calipers.

The V-Max's shaft final drive is a relic from the engine's touring heritage. A similar V-four unit was used in the Yamaha Venture heavyweight tourer launched in 1983.

A small instrument panel on top of the airbox cover holds the indicator lights, tachometer and engine temperature gauge. The single dial on the handlebars is the speedometer.

The chrome 'intake scoops' are merely cosmetic fakes. The real air intake is below the tank cover.

Not all markets enjoyed the full-power 104kw (140bhp) V-Max. Most European countries were supplied with restricted 75kw (100bhp) versions, with the V-Boost carburettor linking system disabled.

Japanese cruiser-type machines have long looked to American machinery for inspiration, but Yamaha's V-Max went a step further, being designed in California. One of the longest-running models in Yamaha's range, it offers an impressive level of performance - in a straight line at least.

When it debuted in 1984, the V-Max's 1198cc (73ci) V-four engine was amazingly powerful, peaking at 104kw (140bhp). This figure was achieved with the help of a curious intake system, dubbed 'V-Boost'. This allowed each individual cylinder to draw fuel and air simultaneously from two

The insubstantial nature of the steel-tube frame can be seen with the fuel tank cover and side panels removed.

carburettors at high engine speeds. Apart from this feature, the rest of the engine is pretty conventional, with four valves per cylinder, four camshafts and a five-speed gearbox with shaft final drive.

IMPERFECT TECHNOLOGY

However, the V-Max engine was just too powerful for its rather low-tech chassis. Japanese chassis technology in the early 1980s was rather imperfect, and the V-Max's steel-tube cradle frame, skinny front forks and twin rear shocks are quickly overwhelmed by cornering forces. Similarly, the original single-piston front brake calipers offered notably poor stopping power, although these were replaced by twin-piston items in 1993. Both front and rear tyres are narrow, high-profile types, which do not offer the handling finesse of wider, modern radial rubber.

But despite these chassis shortcomings, the V-Max is a satisfying machine to ride. In a straight line, the engine provides breathtaking performance, with a surfeit of low-down torque, as well as an impressive top-end rush when the V-Boost system switches in – as it does around 6000rpm. The styling is also attractive, in a suitably brutal fashion: the black-painted engine emphasizes the hunched and aggressive appearance of the V-Max.

Yamaha VMX1200 V-Max

Top speed:	232km/h (144mph)
Engine type:	1198cc (73ci), l/c 90° V-four, 16-valve, DOHC
Max power:	104kw (140bhp) @ 8500rpm
Frame type:	steel-tube double cradle
Tyre sizes:	front 110/90 18, rear 150/90 15
Final drive:	shaft
Gearbox:	five-speed
Weight:	262kg (576lb)

JAPAN

Index

Page numbers in *italics* refer to illustrations